CUSTOMISE YOUR MOBILE!

RINGTONE MANIA! PLATINUM

Exclusive distributors:
Music Sales Limited
8/9 Frith Street, London W1D 3JB, England.
Music Sales Pty Limited
120 Rothschild Avenue, Rosebery, NSW 2018, Australia.

Order No. AM974149   ISBN 0-7119-9441-2
This book © Copyright 2002 by Wise Publications.

Unauthorised reproduction of any part of this publication by any
means including photocopying is an infringement of copyright.

Ringtones arranged by Jonny Lattimer, Lucy Holliday,
Sarah Holcroft, Scott Brown and David Weston.
Compiled by Nick Crispin.
Cover and book design by Phil Gambrill.
Book setting and layout by Simon Troup.
With special thanks to Robin Pickard.
Photographs courtesy of London Features International,
Rex Features and Ronald Grant Archive.
Printed in Malta by Interprint Ltd.

Music Sales' complete catalogue describes thousands of
titles and is available in full colour sections by subject, direct from
Music Sales Limited. Please state your areas of interest and
a cheque/postal order for £1.50 f
Newmarket Roa

This pub
sale in t

WISE PUBLICATIONS
London / New York / Sydney / Paris / Copenhagen / Berlin / Madrid / Tokyo

ENTERTAINMENT

CHART HITS

4

THIS BOOK CONTAINS OVER 200 GREAT TUNES FOR YOU TO PROGRAM INTO YOUR MOBILE PHONE.

Just follow these four simple steps to customise your mobile:

1 Check that your phone has a **COMPOSER** or **RINGTONE EDIT** function (refer to the list of makes and model numbers on pages 120-128) and locate this function on your phone.

2 Refer to pages 120-128 to find **INSTRUCTIONS** on how to program ringtones into your phone. Check your instruction manual for further details on the individual operation of phones.

3 Choose the **TUNE** that you want to program from one of the four sections in this book.

4 GET RINGING!

NOTE: You will get the best results from this book if you have a Nokia mobile phone. Samsung, Siemens and Ericsson models have composer features but, due to differences in the options available on those phones, some melodies will work better than others.

Choose your own ringtone!
E-mail us your ringtone suggestions on **ringtones@musicsales.co.uk**

THE BIG MATCH
By Keith Mansfield

© Copyright 1968 KPM Music Limited, 127 Charing Cross Road, London WC2H OQY.
All Rights Reserved. International Copyright Secured.

F2 8	A#2 8	D#3 8	D3 4	C3 8			TEMPO 160
C3 8	A#2 4	G#2 8	G#2 8	G2 8	F2 4	D#2 4	A#1 8	C2 8
A#1 8	D2 8	F2 2	- 8	- 4	- 2	- 8	F2 8	A#2 8
D#3 8	C#3 4	C3 8	C3 8	A#2 4	G#2 8	G#2 8	G2 8	F2 4
D#2 4	A#1 8	C2 8	A#1 8	D2 8	F2 4	- 8	A#1 8	- 8
- 4	A#1 8	- 8	- 8	A#1 8			

GRANDSTAND
By Keith Mansfield

© Copyright 1975 KPM Music Limited, 127 Charing Cross Road, London WC2H OQY.
All Rights Reserved. International Copyright Secured.

F2 8	A#2 8	D#3 8	D3 4	C3 8			TEMPO 160
C3 8	A#2 4	G#2 8	G#2 8	G2 8	F2 4	D#2 4	A#1 8	C2 8
A#1 8	D2 8	F2 2	- 8	- 4	- 2	- 8	F2 8	A#2 8
D#3 8	C#3 4	C3 8	C3 8	A#2 4	G#2 8	G#2 8	G2 8	F2 4
D#2 4	A#1 8	C2 8	A#1 8	D2 8	F2 4	- 8	A#1 8	- 8
- 4	A#1 8	- 8	- 8	A#1 8			

HORSE OF THE YEAR SHOW
['A MUSICAL JOKE']
By Wolfgang Amadeus Mozart

© Copyright 2002 Dorsey Brothers Music Limited, 8/9 Frith Street, London W1D 3JB.
All Rights Reserved. International Copyright Secured.

| C2 16 | C2 16 | C2 16 | - 16 | A1 16 | | | TEMPO 112 |
| D2 16 | C2 16 | A#1 16 | A1 16 | G1 16 | | | |

(row 2)

A1 16	A1 16	- 16	D2 16	D2 16	C2 16	A#1 16	A1 16	G1 16
- 16	A1 16	A1 16	A1 16	- 16	F1 16	F1 16	F1 16	- 16
A#1 16	A#1 16	A1 16	G1 16	F1 16	E1 16	D1 16	- 16	D2 16
D2 16	C2 16	A#1 16	A1 16	G1 16	F1 16			

LONDON MARATHON ['THE TRAP']
By Ron Goodwin

© Copyright 1966 Filmusic Publishing Company Limited.
Universal/Dick James Music Limited, Elsinore House,
77 Fulham Palace Road, London W6 8JA.
All Rights Reserved. International Copyright Secured.

C1 4	F1 2	G1 4	A1 2	C2 4			TEMPO 180
A1 4.	A#1 8	G1 4	F1 1	- 4	G1 4	A1 4.	A#1 8	C2 4
D2 4.	C2 8	A#1 4	A1 4.	G1 8	F1 1	G1 4	- 4	C1 4
F1 2	G1 4	A1 2	C2 4	A1 4.	A#1 8	G1 4	F1 1	- 4
A1 4	G1 2	E1 4	F1 4.	E1 8	D1 4	C1 2.		

SPORTSMASTER
By Robert Busby

© Copyright 1951 Marlowlynn Limited.
Chappell Recorded Music Library Limited, 10-11 St. Martin's Court, London WC2N 4AL.
All Rights Reserved. International Copyright Secured.

B1 16	C2 16	C#2 16	D2 16	D#2 16			TEMPO 160
E2 16	F2 2	E2 8	A1 4.	A1 8.	A#1 16	C2 2	C2 8.	D2 16
C2 4	A#1 8.	C2 16	A#1 4	A1 8.	A#1 16	A1 2	G1 8	C2 16
C2 16	C2 8	C2 8	F2 2	E2 8	A1 4.	A1 8.	B1 16	C#2 4.
A1 16	A1 16	A1 16	F1 16	A1 16	B1 16	C2 8	C2 16	C2 16
C2 16	A1 16	C2 16	E2 16	G2 4	G2 4	A2 32	B2 32	C3 8

SPORTS REPORT ['OUT OF THE BLUE']
By Hubert Bath

© Copyright 1931 B. Feldman & Company Limited,
127 Charing Cross Road, London WC2H 0GY.
All Rights Reserved. International Copyright Secured.

A1 16	A1 8	A#1 16	A#1 16	- 16		TEMPO 90
A1 16	A1 16	- 16	G1 16	G1 16	- 16	A1 16	A1 16	A#1 16
A1 16	G1 16	- 8	A#1 16	A1 8	- 4	A1 16	A#1 16	A1 16
G1 16	- 8	A#1 16	A1 8	- 8	G1 16	A1 16	G1 16	FL 8
- 16	A1 16	G1 8

SPORTSNIGHT

By Tony Hatch

© Copyright 1970 Mr & Mrs Music Limited/Dejamus Limited,
Suite 11, Accurist House, 44 Baker Street, London W1U 7AZ.
All Rights Reserved. International Copyright Secured.

A2 4	A#2 8	A#2 4	A2 8	F2 8			TEMPO 125
D2 8	A1 4	A#1 8	A#1 4	A1 8	F1 8	D1 8	A2 4	A#2 8
A#2 4	A2 8	F2 8	D2 8	A1 8	A#1 4	A#1 8	A1 8	F1 8
D1 8	F1 8	C1 8	D#1 4	F1 8	C1 8	D#1 8	F1 8	A#1 8
F1 8	G#1 8	A#1 4	F1 8	G#1 8	A#1 8	C2 8	G1 8	A#1 8
C2 4	G1 8	A#1 8	C2 8	C2 8			

TEST CRICKET ['SOUL LIMBO']

By Booker T. Jones, Steve Cropper, Al Jackson & Donald 'Duck' Dunn

© Copyright 1968 East Memphis Music Corporation/Irving Music Incorporated, USA.
Rondor Music (London) Limited, 10A Parsons Green, London SW6 4TW.
All Rights Reserved. International Copyright Secured.

G1 8	G1 8	G1 8	G1 16	A1 8			TEMPO 125
A1 16	A1 8	A1 16	A1 8	A1 16	B1 8	B1 8	B1 8	B1 16
A1 16	- 8	G1 8	A1 16	C1 8	A1 16	C2 4	- 2	- 4
- 8	A1 8.	C2 8.	F2 8.	E2 8.	D2 16.	D2 32	D#2 32	E2 8.
C2 16							

TOUR DE FRANCE
By Ralf Hutter, Florian Schneider-Esleben & Karl Bartos

© Copyright 1983 Kling Klang Musik GmbH/Hanseatic Musikverlag GmbH, Germany.
Sony/ATV Music Publishing (UK) Limited,
10 Great Marlborough Street, London W1F 7LP (75%)/Copyright Control (25%).
All Rights Reserved. International Copyright Secured.

F1 4	A#1 8	C2 8	F2 4.	D2 8			TEMPO 125
F2 8	G2 8	C2 8	D2 8	F2 4	A#2 1	G#2 1	- 1	F1 4
A#1 8	C2 8	F2 4.	D2 8	F2 8	G2 8	C2 8	D2 8	F2 4
A#2 4	C3 1	- 1	G1 4	C2 8	D2 8	G2 4.	E2 8	G2 8
A2 8	D2 8	E2 8	G2 4	C3 4	A#2 1		

WE'RE ON THE BALL
[OFFICIAL ENGLAND WORLD CUP SONG 2002]
Words & Music by Harold Spiro, Anthony McPartlin & Declan Donnelly

© Copyright 2002 Trekfarm Limited / The Music & Media Partnership Limited /
Sony/ATV Music Publishing (UK) Limited, 10 Great Marlborough Street, London W1F 7LP
All Rights Reserved. International Copyright Secured.

C2 8	E2 16	G2 16	E2 16	G2 16			TEMPO 112
E2 16	C2 8	C2 8	C2 8	C2 16	C2 8	C2 8	C2 16	C2 8
C2 16	C2 16	C2 8	A1 8	A1 8	A1 16	A1 8	A1 8	A1 16
A1 8	A1 16	A1 16	B1 8	B1 8	B1 8	B1 16	B1 8	B1 8
B1 16	B1 8	B1 16	B1 16	B1 8	G1 8	G1 8	G1 16	G1 8
C2 8	E2 16	G2 16	E2 16	G2 16	E2 16	C2 4		

WIMBLEDON CLOSING THEME
['SPORTING OCCASION']
By Arnold Steck

© Copyright 1959 Marlowlynn Limited.
Chappell Recorded Music Library Limited, 10-11 St. Martin's Court, London WC2N 4AL.
All Rights Reserved. International Copyright Secured.

C2 2.	D#1 2.	F1 4	G1 8	F1 4			TEMPO 200
G1 8	#D1 4	C1 8	D#1 4	G#1 8	C2 2.	C#2 4	C2 8	A#1 4
C2 8	D#2 8	D#2 16	D#2 16	D#2 8	D#2 8	D#2 8	D#2 8	D#2 8
F1 8	G1 8	G#1 8	A#1 8	C2 2.	C#2 2.	D#1 4	F1 8	G1 8
F1 4	G1 8	D#1 4	A#1 8	C2 4	C#2 8	F2 2.	G2 4.	F2 4.
D#2 8	D#2 16	D#2 16	D#2 8	D#2 8	D#2 8	D#2 8	D#2 4.	D#1 4.

WORLD IN MOTION
[OFFICIAL ENGLAND WORLD CUP SONG 1990]
Words & Music by Peter Hook, Stephen Morris, Bernard Sumner, Gillian Gilbert & Keith Allen

© Copyright 1990 Gainwest Limited/Warner/Chappell Music Limited, Griffin House,
London W6 8BS (62.5%)/EMI Music Publishing Limited, London WC2H 0QY (37.5%).
All Rights Reserved. International Copyright Secured.

F#1 4	F#1 8	D#1 8	F#1 4	D#1 8			TEMPO 125
G#1 8	- 8	D#1 4	F#1 8	- 8	B1 8	- 8	A#1 8	- 8
G#1 8	- 8	F#1 8	- 8	G#1 8	- 4	D#1 2	C#1 4	- 8
F#1 4	F#1 8	D#1 8	F#1 4	D#1 8	G#1 8	- 8	D#1 4	F#1 8
- 8	B1 8	- 8	A#1 8	- 8	G#1 8	- 8	F#1 8	- 8
G#1 8	- 4	D#1 2	C#1 4				

ANIMAL MAGIC
By Laurie Johnson

© Copyright 1960 KPM Music Limited, 127 Charing Cross Road, London WC2H 0QY.
All Rights Reserved. International Copyright Secured.

A1 16	- 16	G1 16	- 16	C1 16		TEMPO 112
C1 16	- 16	C1 16	C1 16	- 16	D1 16	- 16	E1 16	- 8
- 16	A1 16	- 16	G1 16	- 16	D1 16	D1 16	- 16	E1 16
F1 16	- 4	- 8	- 16	A1 16	- 16	G1 16	- 16	D1 16
D1 16	- 16	D1 16	D1 16	- 16	E1 16	- 16	F1 16	- 8
- 16	A1 16	- 16	G1 16	- 16	C1 16	C1 8	D1 16	E1 16

THE AVENGERS
By Laurie Johnson

© Copyright 1965 EMI Film & Theatre Music Limited,
127 Charing Cross Road, London WC2H 0QY.
All Rights Reserved. International Copyright Secured.

G1 2	- 8	C#2 16	- 16	D2 16		TEMPO 160
- 16	F#2 8.	G2 2	- 8	G2 2	- 8	C#3 16	- 16	D3 16
- 16	F#3 8.	G3 2	- 8	G1 2.	E1 4	F1 2	A#1 4	D2 4
C2 2.	G1 4	E1 4	F1 2	- 4	G1 2.	E1 4	F1 2	A#1 4
D2 4	E2 2.	C2 4	C#2 4	D2 2.

BLIND DATE
By Laurie Holloway

© Copyright 1985 Standard Music Limited, Onward House,
11 Uxbridge Street, London W8 7TQ.
All Rights Reserved. International Copyright Secured.

A#1 16	- 4	C2 8.	A#1 16	- 4			TEMPO 112
C2 8.	A#1 8	C2 8	A#1 16	C2 8	A#1 16	- 4	F2 8.	D#2 16
- 4	F2 8.	D#2 16	- 4	F2 8.	D#2 8	F2 8	D#2 16	F2 8
D#2 16	- 4	C2 8.	A#1 16	- 4	C2 8.	A#1 16	- 4	C2 8.
A#1 8	C2 8	A#1 16	C2 8	C#2 16	- 4	C2 8.	D#2 16	- 4
C2 8.	D#2 16	- 4	C2 8.	D#2 8	C2 8	D#2 16	F2 8	D#2 16

CHARLIE'S ANGELS
By Allyn Ferguson & Jack Elliott

© Copyright 1977 EMI Gold Horizon Music Corporation/Spellgold Music, USA.
EMI Music Publishing Limited, 127 Charing Cross Road, London WC2H OGY.
All Rights Reserved. International Copyright Secured.

C#2 4	D2 8	C#2 2	B1 4	E2 4	D2 4	C#2 4	TEMPO 160
D2 8	C#2 2	- 8	D2 8	B1 8	C#2 8	D2 8	E2 8	F#2 4
G2 8	F#2 2	E2 4	A2 4	G2 4	F#2 1			
- 2	B1 4	C2 8	B1 2	A1 4	F#1 8			
B1 2	G1 8	A1 8	B1 4	C2 8	A1 4			
D2 4	C2 4	B1 1						

DICK BARTON ['DEVIL'S GALOP']

By Charles Williams

© Copyright 1944 Chappell & Company Limited.
Rights assigned 1988 to Marlowlynn Limited/
Chappell Recorded Music Library Limited, 165-167 High Road, London NW10 2SG.
All Rights Reserved. International Copyright Secured.

D1 8	C#1 16	A1 16	D#1 8	F1 16		TEMPO 180	
D#1 16	D1 8	C#1 16	D1 16	D#1 8	F1 16	D#1 16	D1 8	E1 8
F#1 8	G1 8	F#1 8	G1 8	A1 8	A#1 8	C2 8	B1 16	A#1 16
A1 8	C2 8	A#1 8	A1 8	C2 8	D#2 8	D2 32	D#2 32	D2 32
D#2 32	D2 32	D#2 32	D2 32	D#2 32	D2 32	D#2 32	D2 32	D#2 32
D2 32	D#2 32	D2 32	D#2 32	D2 32	D#2 32	D2 32	D#2 32	D2 2

FRASIER

Words & Music by Bruce Miller & Darryl Phinnessee

© Copyright 1993 Bruin Music Company/Famous Music Corporation, USA.
All Rights Reserved. International Copyright Secured.

F1 8	G1 8	A#1 8	C2 8	C#2 4		TEMPO 200	
D2 8	A#1 4	F1 8	E1 4	C#2 4.	A#1 8	C2 4	D#2 4.	C2 8
A#1 4.	G1 4	F1 2	- 4	F1 8	G1 8	A#1 8	C2 8	C#2 8
- 8	C#2 8	A#1 8	- 8	A#1 8	G#1 8	- 8	F1 2	D#1 8
- 8	D#1 8	- 8	C1 8	- 8	C1 8			

LAUREL & HARDY
['DANCE OF THE CUCKOOS']
By T. Marvin Hatley

© Copyright 1930 & 1932 Hatley Music Company, USA.
Robert Kingston (Music) Limited, 8/9 Frith Street, London W1D 3JB.
All Rights Reserved. International Copyright Secured.

A1	G2	G#2	A2	C3				TEMPO
32	32	32	8	16				100

A2	-	A1	G2	G#2	A2	C3	A2	
16	32	32	32	32	8	16	8	16

A#2	C3	A#2	G2	-	G2	A#2	A2	F2
16	16	16	8	16	16	16	16	16

-	A1	G2	G#2	A2	C3	A2	-	A1
32	32	32	32	8	16	16	16	32

G2	G#2	A2	C3	A2	-	A#2	C3	A#2
32	32	8	16	8	16	16	16	16

G2	C3	F2
8	16	8.

PINGU
By Antonio Conde

© Copyright 1993 GEMA/Copyright Control.
All Rights Reserved. International Copyright Secured.

C2	A1	A#1	A1	G1				TEMPO
4	4	8	8	4				112

C2	A1	A#1	D2	C2	D2	F2	E2	D2
4	4	8	8	4	8	8	8	8

C2	F2	C2	A#1	A1	A#1	A1	G1	C2
8	8	8	8	8	8	8	8	4

-	A#1	A1	C2	F2
8	8	4	4	4

PLEASE SIR
By Sam Fonteyn

© Copyright 1968 Standard Music Limited, Onward House,
11 Uxbridge Street, London W8 7TQ.
All Rights Reserved. International Copyright Secured.

D#2 **8**	E2 **16**	- **8**	D#2 **16**	E2 **8**		TEMPO **125**
- **16**	C2 **8.**	A1 **4**	- **16**	C2 **4**	- **8**	- **16**	D#2 **8**	E2 **16**
- **8**	D#2 **16**	E2 **8.**	C2 **8.**	F2 **8.**	E2 **8**	D2 **4**	- **8**	- **16**
D#2 **8**	E2 **16**	- **8**	D#2 **16**	E2 **8**	- **16**	C2 **8.**	A1 **4**	- **16**
C2 **4**	- **8**	- **16**	E2 **8**	D#2 **16**	D2 **8**	C#2 **4**	D2 **8**	C2 **16**
B1 **8**	C2 **16**	D2 **8**	C2 **4**			

SABRINA, THE TEENAGE WITCH
By Danny Lux & Paul Taylor

© Copyright 1998 Viacom Music, USA.
BMG Music Publishing Limited, Bedford House,
69-79 Fulham High Street, London SW6 3JW.
All Rights Reserved. International Copyright Secured.

D2 **4.**	D2 **4.**	B1 **8**	C2 **8**	D2 **4**		TEMPO **160**
C2 **4**	B1 **8.**	A1 **8.**	G1 **8**	C2 **32**	D2 **4**	C2 **4.**	A1 **8**	A#1 **8**
C2 **4**	A#1 **4**	A1 **4**	G1 **4**	G1 **16**	- **16**	- **32**	D2 **32**	E2 **4**
D2 **4.**	B1 **8**	B1 **8**	C2 **8**	D2 **4**	C2 **8**	A#1 **4**	C2 **8**	D2 **8**
- **16**	- **32**	C2 **32**	D2 **2**	- **8**	A#1 **8**	C2 **8**	D2 **2.**

CAGNEY & LACEY [INTRO]

By Bill Conti

© Copyright 1983 Orion Music Publishing Incorporated, USA.
Universal Music Publishing Limited, Elsinore House,
77 Fulham Palace Road, London W6 8JA.
All Rights Reserved. International Copyright Secured.

G2 8	G2 8	F2 8	E2 8	C2 8			TEMPO 125
G1 8	F1 8	E1 8	C1 8	D#1 16	E1 16	G1 16	A1 16	C2 16
D2 16	E2 16	C2 16	A1 16	F1 16	D2 16	B1 16	G1 16	E1 16
C2 8	G2 8	A2 8	B2 4	A2 4	G2 4	E2 8	D2 8	C2 4

SOUTH PARK

Words & Music by Leslie Claypool, Reid Lalonde III & Bryan Mantia

© Copyright 1997 Hilarity Music Incorporated, USA.
4AD Music Limited, 17-19 Alma Road, London SW18 1AA.
All Rights Reserved. International Copyright Secured.

E1 16.	F1 32	F#1 8	E1 16.	F1 32			TEMPO 125
F#1 4	F#1 8	F#1 8	F#1 8	E1 16.	F1 32	F#1 8	E1 16.	F1 32
F#1 16	F#1 4.	- 16	- 8	A1 8	A1 8	A1 8	A1 8	C2 8
C2 8	C2 8	- 8	A1 8	A1 8	A1 8	A1 8	C2 8	C2 8
C2 8	- 8	C2 16	C2 16	C#2 16	- 16	C2 8.	C#2 16	C2 16
C2 16	A1 8	F#1 8	A1 8	C2 8	C#2 8	C2 8.	C#2 16	C2 4.

SPIDER-MAN

Words by Paul Francis Webster
Music by Robert J. Harris

© Copyright 1969 Webster Music Company/Hillcrest Music Corporation, USA.
Rondor Music (London) Limited, 10A Parsons Green, London SW6 4TW (50%)/
Copyright Control (50%). All Rights Reserved. International Copyright Secured.

C1 4	D#1 8	G1 2	- 8	F1 4		TEMPO 200
D#1 8	C1 2	- 8	C1 4	D#1 8	G1 4	G1 4	G1 8	F1 4
D#1 8	C1 2	- 8	F1 4	G#1 8	C2 2	- 8	A#1 4	G#1 8
F1 2	- 8	C1 4	D#1 8	G1 4	G1 4	G1 8	F1 4	D#1 8
C1 4	- 8	G1 8.	F1 4	- 16	- 8	- 2	F1 8	F1 4
D#1 8	F1 4	D#1 8	C1 2

TALES OF THE UNEXPECTED

By Ron Grainer

© Copyright 1979 Westminster Music Limited,
Suite 2.07, Plaza 535 King's Road, London SW10 0SZ.
All Rights Reserved. International Copyright Secured.

G#2 8.	G2 8.	G#2 8.	G#1 16	C2 16		TEMPO 50
D#2 16	G#2 8.	G2 8.	F2 8.	A#1 16	C#2 16	F2 16	G#2 8.	G2 8.
F2 8.	G#1 16	C2 16	D#2 16	G#2 8.	G2 8.	F2 8.	D#2 8.	G#2 8.
A#2 8.	G#2 8.	G#1 16	C2 16	D#2 16	G#2 8.	G2 8.	F2 8.	A#1 16
C#2 16	F2 16	G#2 8.	G2 8.	F2 8.	G#1 16	C2 16	D#2 16	F2 4
G2 4	G#2 2

AMELIE ['LE BANQUET']

By Yann Tiersen

© Copyright 1995 Ici, d'ailleurs.../Sony Music Publishing, France.
Sony/ATV Music Publishing (UK) Limited, 10 Great Marlborough Street, London W1F 7LP.
All Rights Reserved. International Copyright Secured.

A1 4	B1 4	C2 8	B1 8	A1 2			TEMPO 180
C2 8	B1 8	A1 2	G1 8	F#1 8	E1 2	- 8	F#1 8	G1 8
A1 8	B1 8	D2 8	C2 8	B1 8	A1 2	C2 8	B1 8	A1 2
B1 1	C2 4	E2 8	D2 8	C2 2	E2 8	D2 8	C2 2	B1 8
A1 8	G1 2	- 8	F#1 8	G1 8	A1 8	B1 8	D2 8	E2 8
D2 8	C2 .2	E2 8	D2 8	C2 2	B1 1			

THE BIG COUNTRY

By Jerome Moross

© Copyright 1958 United Artists Music Company Incorporated/Chappell &
Company Incorporated, USA. Warner/Chappell Music Limited, Griffin House,
161 Hammersmith Road, London W6 8BS.
All Rights Reserved. International Copyright Secured.

A1 4	F#1 2	A1 4	D2 4.	E2 8			TEMPO 180
D2 8	E2 8	F#2 4	D2 2	- 2	A1 4	F#1 2	A1 4	D2 4.
E2 8	D2 8	F#2 8	E2 2.	- 2	A1 4	F#1 2	A1 4	D2 4.
E2 8	D2 8	E2 8	F#2 4	D2 2	B1 2	D2 4	F#2 2	D2 4
B1 4.	A1 8	C#2 8	E2 8	D2 2.				

THE ALAMO
By Dimitri Tiomkin

© Copyright 1960 Volta Music Corporation, USA.
BMG Music Publishing Limited, Bedford House,
69-79 Fulham High Street, London SW6 3JW.
All Rights Reserved. International Copyright Secured.

A1 4	D2 4.	E2 8	D2 8	C#2 4			**TEMPO 160**
A1 4	A1 4	D2 4.	C#2 8	D2 4	E2 4	C2 4	F2 4.	E2 8
F2 4	G2 4	D2 4	G2 4	G#2 4	E2 4	G#2 4	A2 2	A2 8
A#2 8	C3 4.	A#2 8	A2 4	G2 4	D2 4	G2 8	A2 8	A#2 4.
A2 8	G2 4	F2 4	C2 4	F2 8	G2 8	A2 4.	G2 8	F2 4
E2 4	G2 4	E2 4	D2 4	F2 4	D2 4	E2 2		

THE MATRIX [CLUBBED TO DEATH]
By Rob Dougan

© Copyright 1995 BMG Music Publishing Limited, Bedford House,
69-79 Fulham High Street, London SW6 3JW.
All Rights Reserved. International Copyright Secured.

G1 4	A#1 4	G1 4	C2 4	F#1 4	A1 4	F#1 4	**TEMPO 140**
D2 4	A#1 4	D2 4	A#1 4	A#1 4	A1 4	C2 2	
G1 4	A#1 4	D2 4	G2 2.	G2 4			
G2 2.	F2 4	F2 2	D#2 2	D2 4			
D1 4	G1 4	A#1 4	A#1 2	A1 2			
G1 1							

CYRANO DE BERGERAC
By Jean-Claude Petit

© Copyright 1989 Art Music/Hachette Company, France/SDRM.
All Rights Reserved. International Copyright Secured.

D1 16	G1 8.	A#1 16	D2 4	- 8			TEMPO 70
- 16	G2 16	A#2 8.	A2 16	D2 4	- 8	- 16	F2 16	D#2 8.
D2 16	A1 4	- 8	- 16	C2 16	A#1 8.	A1 16	G1 8.	F#1 16
E1 32	F#1 32	E1 8	D1 16	G1 8.	A#1 16	D2 4	- 8	- 16
G2 16	A#2 8.	A2 16	F2 4	- 8	- 16	D2 16	A1 8.	F2 16
D2 8.	A1 16	F1 32	G1 32	F1 8	E1 16	D1 2		

WITNESS [BUILDING THE BARN]
By Maurice Jarre

© Copyright 1985 Famous Music Corporation, USA.
All Rights Reserved. International Copyright Secured.

B2 8	B1 8	D2 8	B1 8	G2 8			TEMPO 90
D2 8	B2 8	G2 8	C3 8	C2 8	E2 8	C2 8	G2 8	E2 8
C3 8	G2 8	D3 8	D2 8	F#2 8	D2 8	A2 8	D3 8	C3 8
D3 8	D2 8	E2 8	G2 4	G2 4	B2 8	A2 4	A2 8	G2 4
G2 8	A2 8	B2 8	A2 4	A2 8	F#2 8	E2 8	D2 4	

1492: CONQUEST OF PARADISE

By Vangelis

© Copyright 1992 Spheric B.V./EMI Music Publishing Limited,
127 Charing Cross Road, London WC2H OQY.
All Rights Reserved. International Copyright Secured.

A1 8	F2 8.	E2 16	D2 4	C#2 8			TEMPO 90
D2 8	E2 8.	C#2 16	A1 4.	A1 8	F2 8.	E2 16	D2 4	C#2 8
D2 8	E2 2	C2 4	A2 8.	G2 16	F2 4	E2 8	F2 8	G2 8.
E2 16	C2 4.	C2 8	A#1 8.	C2 16	D2 4	C2 8	A#1 8	A1 2

HALLOWE'EN

By John Carpenter

© Copyright 1978 Jack-O'-Lantern Music Publishing Company, USA.
Screen Music Services Limited, 32 Lexington Street, London W1F OLQ.
All Rights Reserved. International Copyright Secured.

C#2 8	F#1 8	F#1 8	C#2 8	F#1 8			TEMPO 140
F#1 8	C#2 8	F#1 8	D2 8	F#1 8	C#2 8	F#1 8	F#1 8	C#2 8
F#1 8	F#1 8	C#2 8	F#1 8	D2 8	F#1 8	C2 8	F1 8	F1 8
C2 8	F1 8	F1 8	C2 8	F1 8	C#2 8	F1 8	C2 8	F1 8
F1 8	C2 8	F1 8	F1 8	C2 8	F1 8	C#2 8	F1 8	C2 8
F1 8	F1 8	C2 8	F1 8	F1 8	C2 8	F1 8	C#2 8	F1 8

YELLOW SUBMARINE
[HEY BULLDOG]

Words & Music by John Lennon & Paul McCartney

© Copyright 1968 Northern Songs.
All Rights Reserved. International Copyright Secured.

C1 8	C1 8	D#1 8	C1 16	F1 8		TEMPO 100
C1 16	F#1 8	C1 8	G1 8	C1 8	C1 8	D#1 8 · C1 16 · G1 8
C1 16	F#1 8	C1 8	F1 8	C1 8	C1 8	D#1 8 · C1 16 · F1 8
C1 16	F#1 4	G1 8	G1 8	G1 8	A#1 8	G1 16 · D2 8 · G1 16
C#2 4	A#1 8	C1 8	C1 8	D#1 8	C1 16	F1 8 · C1 16 · F#1 4
G1 8	G1 8	G1 8	A#1 8	G1 16	D2 8	G1 16 · C#2 4 · C2 8

TAXI DRIVER
By Bernard Herrmann

© Copyright 1976 Screen Gems-EMI Music Incorporated, USA.
Screen Gems-EMI Music Limited, 127 Charing Cross Road, London WC2H 0QY.
All Rights Reserved. International Copyright Secured.

A#1 4	C2 16	D2 16	D#2 16	F2 16		TEMPO 140
G2 16	G2 32	A2 4	G2 1	A2 8	A2 32	C3 8 · A2 2. · G2 8.
G2 4.	F2 2.	G2 8	G2 32	A2 8	G2 2.	F2 4 · A#2 32 · C3 4.
A2 4.	C3 4.	D#3 4	D#3 8.	D#3 4	D3 32	D#3 4 · D3 4 · C#3 4
C3 8	E3 8	C3 2				

A MAN AND A WOMAN
[UN HOMME ET UNE FEMME]

Music by Francis Lai. Original Words by Pierre Barouh
English Words by Jerry Keller

© Copyright 1966 Editions Saravah, France. Universal/MCA Music Limited, London W6 8JA
for the British Commonwealth, the Republic of Ireland and South Africa.
All Rights Reserved. International Copyright Secured.

A#1 2	C2 2	C#2 2	D2 8	D2 8			TEMPO 160
D2 8	D2 8	D2 8	-	D2 8	D2 8	D2 8	D2 8	D2 8
- 4	- 8	C2 4	D2 4	D#2 4	D2 8	D2 8	D2 8	D2 8
D2 8	- 8	D2 8	D2 8	D2 8	D2 8	D2 8	- 4	- 8
C2 4	D2 4	D#2 4	C2 8	C2 8	C2 8	C2 8	C2 8	- 8
C2 8	C2 8	C2 8	C2 8	C2 8	A#1 2	C2 4	C#2 4	C2 1

CHOCOLAT [PASSAGE OF TIME]

By Rachel Portman

© Copyright 2000 Miramax Film Music, USA.
Sony/ATV Music Publishing (UK) Limited, 10 Great Marlborough Street, London W1F 7LP.
All Rights Reserved. International Copyright Secured.

E3 16	- 16	D#3 16	E3 16	C3 16			TEMPO 90
- 16	B2 16	- 16	A#2 16	B2 16	G2 16	- 16	F#2 16	- 16
E2 16	D#2 16	- 16	-	B1 16	C#2 16	D#2 16	- 16	D#2 16
E2 16	F#2 16	- 16	F#2 16	G2 16	A2 16	- 16	B2 16	- 16
E3 16	- 16	- 8	B1 16	A1 16	G1 16	F#1 16	E1 16	- 16
B2 32	C3 32	C#3 32	D#2 32	E3 4

ZOOLANDER [ROCKIT]

By Herbie Hancock, Bill Laswell & Michael Beinhorn©

© Copyright 1983 Hancock Music Company/More Cut Music, USA.
Sony/ATV Music Publishing (UK) Limited, 10 Great Marlborough Street,
London W1F 7LP (33.34%)/Copyright Control (66.66%).
All Rights Reserved. International Copyright Secured.

A1 8	B1 8	- 4	E1 8	C2 8				TEMPO 112
- 4	E1 8	D#2 8.	D2 8.	C2 4	- 16	A1 8	E1 16	G1 16
- 4	D2 8	C2 8	- 8	G1 16	- 16	G1 16	A1 16	- 1
A1 8	B1 8	- 4	E1 8	C2 8	- 4	E1 8	D#2 8.	D2 8.
C2 4	- 16	A1 8	E1 16	G1 16	- 4	D2 8	C2 8	- 8
G1 16	- 16	G1 16	A1 16					

OCEAN'S ELEVEN [69 POLICE]

By David Holmes, Phil Mossman, Darren Morris, Italo Salizzato, Aldo Tagliapietra, Stanley Walden & Giovanni Smeraldi

© Copyright 2000 Universal/Island Music Limited, London W6 8JA (30%)/ EMI Unart
Catalog Incorporated, worldwide print rights controlled by Warner Bros. Publishing
Incorporated/IMP Limited (10%)/White Noise/Suono Edizioni Musicali & C.A. Rossi Editore,
Italy/SIAE (50%)/Copyright Control (10%).All Rights Reserved. International Copyright Secured.

A1 4	E2 4	A2 4	E2 4	A2 4				TEMPO 225
E2 4	A2 4	E2 4	A2 4	G2 2	D2 4	G2 4	D2 4	G2 4
D2 4	G2 4	F#2 4	F#2 4	E2 4	E2 4	D2 4	D2 4	C#2 4
D2 4	C#2 4	D2 4	C#2 4	B1 4				
A1 2								

THE PRODUCERS
[SPRINGTIME FOR HITLER]
Words & Music by Mel Brooks

© Copyright 1968 Legation Music Corporation, USA.
BMG Music Publishing Limited, Bedford House, 69-79 Fulham High Street, London SW6 3JW.
All Rights Reserved. International Copyright Secured.

D2 8	D1 4	D2 8	C2 8	D1 4				TEMPO 80
C2 8	B1 8	D2 16	B1 8.	- 2	- 8	D2 8	D1 4	D2 8
C2 8	D1 4	C2 8	B1 2					

SUSPIRIA
By Claudio Simonetti, Franco Pignatelli,
Massimo Morante & Antonio Marangolo

© Copyright 1976 Edizioni Bixio C.E.M.S.A., Italy.
Edward Kassner Music Company Limited, Units 6 & 7, 11 Wyfold Road, London SW6 6SE.
All Rights Reserved. International Copyright Secured.

D1 16	D1 16	D1 16	E1 16	E1 16			TEMPO 90
E1 16	F1 16	F1 16	F1 16	A1 16	A1 16	A1 16	G1 16	G1 16
G1 16	F1 16	F1 16	F1 16	G1 4	- 8	F1 16	F1 16	F1 16
G1 16	G1 16	G1 16	A1 16	A1 16	A1 16	D1 16	D1 16	D1 16
D1 4								

DEVDAS [BAIRI PIYA]

Music by Ismail Darbar
Lyrics by Nusrat Badr

© Copyright 2002 Universal Music India Limited.
Universal Music Publishing Limited, Elsinore House, 77 Fulham Palace Road,
London W6 8JA. All Rights Reserved. International Copyright Secured.

C2 8	C2 16	C2 16	C2 8	B1 8			TEMPO 140
C2 8	E2 8	C2 8	B1 8	A1 8	A1 16	A1 16	A1 8	G#1 8
A1 4	G#1 4	A1 8	A1 16	A1 16	A1 8	G#1 8	A1 8	C2 8
A1 8	G1 8	F1 8	F1 16	F1 16	F1 8	E1 8	F1 4	E1 4
F1 8	F1 16	F1 16	F1 8	A1 8	D2 16	C2 16	A1 16	G1 16
C2 16	A1 16	G1 16	F1 16	D1 4.	C1 8	D1 4.	C1 8	D1 4

BOMBAY THEME

By A.R. Rahman

© Copyright 1994 PolyGram India Limited.
Universal Music Publishing Limited, Elsinore House,
77 Fulham Palace Road, London W6 8JA.
All Rights Reserved. International Copyright Secured.

A2 8.	A2 8.	A2 8	A2 8.	A2 8.			TEMPO 90
A2 8	G2 16	A2 16	B2 32	A2 32	B2 8.	A2 8	G2 4	F2 16
E2 16	D2 8	D2 8	F2 32	G2 32	A2 8.	A2 8	A2 8.	A2 8.
A2 8	G2 16	A2 16	B2 32	A2 32	B2 8.	A2 8	G2 4	F2 16
E2 16	D2 8	E2 8.	G2 32	A2 8.	G2 8	F2 8.	E2 8	E2 32
F2 32	E2 32.	D2 4

SAAJAN [DEKHA HAI PEHLI BAAR]

Music by Nadeem Shravan
Lyrics by Sameer

© Copyright 1991 PolyGram India Limited.
Universal Music Publishing Limited, Elsinore House, 77 Fulham Palace Road, London W6 8JA.
All Rights Reserved. International Copyright Secured.

A1 4	A1 8	A1 8	A1 4	A1 4				TEMPO 225
E2 2	E2 2	D2 4	C2 4	B1 4	C2 4	A1 4	A1 8	A1 8
A1 4	A1 4	E2 2	E2 2	D2 4	C2 4	B1 4	A1 4	G1 4
G1 8	G1 8	G1 4	G1 4	D2 2	D2 4	E2 4	F2 4	E2 4
D2 2	C2 4	B1 2	D2 4	C2 4	B1 4	A1 2	G1 4	A1 2

DIL TO PAGAL HAI

Music by Uttam Singh
Lyrics by Anand Bakshi

© Copyright 1997 Saregama India Limited. Saregama PLC,
Unit 3, Bush Industrial Estate, Standard Road, Park Royal, London NW10 6HD.
All Rights Reserved. International Copyright Secured.

F#1 8	G#1 8	A1 16	B1 8	A1 16				TEMPO 112
B1 8	A1 4.	G#1 8	F#1 8	G#1 16	A1 16	G#1 16	F#1 16	G#1 8
C#2 8	G#1 2	A1 32	B1 32	C#2 32	D2 4.	C#2 16	D2 16	C#2 4.
B1 16	C#2 16	B1 8	A1 16	B1 16	A1 8	G#1 16	A1 16	G#1 8
F1 32	F#1 32	G#1 32.	F1 8	C#1 8	F#1 4			

KAHO NAA PYAAR HAI

Music by Rajesh Roshan. Lyrics by Ibrahim Ashq

© Copyright 1999 Saregama PLC, Unit 3, Bush Industrial Estate,
Standard Road, Park Royal, London NW10 6HD (50%)/PDA Music Publishing/
Notting Hill Music (UK) Limited, 8B Berkeley Gardens, London W8 4AP (50%).
All Rights Reserved. International Copyright Secured.

C#2 16	- 8	C#2 16.	C#2 16.	E2 32			TEMPO 125	
D2 16.	- 8	C#2 16	- 4	C#2 16.	C#2 16.	C#2 16	E2 32	D2 16.
- 8	C#2 16	- 8	B1 16.	- 8	B1 16.	D2 16.	D2 32	C#2 16.
- 8	B1 8.	B1 8	- 2	F#1 16.	- 8	F#1 16.	G1 16.	A1 16
- 8	A1 8.	B1 8.	C#2 16.	D2 32	C#2 32	B1 8.	A1 16.	G1 16.
G1 16.	- 8	G1 16.	B1 16.	A1 32	B1 32	A1 8	G1 8.	F#1 8.

KEHNA HI KYA [BOMBAY]

Music by A.R. Rahman
Lyrics by Mehboob

© Copyright 1994 PolyGram India Limited. Universal Music Publishing Limited,
Elsinore House, 77 Fulham Palace Road, London W6 8JA.
All Rights Reserved. International Copyright Secured.

A1 16	A1 16	A1 16	C2 16	E2 16			TEMPO 125	
E2 16	E2 16	C2 16	A1 8	E2 8	D2 8	A1 8	- 8	A1 8
A1 16	C2 16	A1 8	C2 8	E1 8	- 8	E2 8	E2 8	E2 8
D2 16	C2 16	E2 32	D2 8	C2 8	B1 8	A1 8	A1 4	A1 16
C2 16	A1 8	B1 8	C2 8	- 8	E2 4	E2 8	D2 16	C2 16
E2 32	D2 8	C2 8	B1 8	A1 8	A1 4	- 8	C2 8	A2 4

ONE TWO KA FOUR
[KHAMOSHIYAN GUNGUANE LAGI]

Music by A.R. Rahman. Lyrics by Majrooh Sultanpuri

© Copyright 2000 Saregama India Limited. Saregama PLC.
Unit 3, Bush Industrial Estate, Standard Road, Park Royal, London NW10 6HD.
All Rights Reserved. International Copyright Secured.

B1 8	D2 8	E2 8	G2 8	F#2 8		TEMPO 180	
G2 8	E2 8.	F2 8.	E2 8.	D2 8.	C#2 8.	D2 8	B1 8.	- 16
G1 8	A1 8	B1 8	D2 8	C#2 8	D2 8.	B1 8	C2 8	B1 8
F#1 8.	G1 8.	C2 8	B1 8.	- 16	A1 8.	- 16	C1 8.	C1 32
C1 32	C1 8	C1 32	C1 32	C1 8	C1 8	D1 8	D1 32	D1 8
E1 8	E1 32	E1 8	D1 8	E1 32	E1 8	D1 8	E1 4

DILWALE DULHANIA LE JAYENGE
[MEHNDI LAGA KE RAKHNA]

Music by Jatin-Lalit. Lyrics by Anand Bakshi

© Copyright 1995 Saregama India Limited. Saregama PLC.
Unit 3, Bush Industrial Estate, Standard Road, Park Royal, London NW10 6HD.
All Rights Reserved. International Copyright Secured.

G1 8	A1 8	A#1 8	C2 8	D2 8.		TEMPO 100	
C2 8.	A#1 16	C2 16	D2 8.	C2 32	D2 32	C2 8	A#1 8	D2 8.
C2 8	- 8	C2 8	C2 16	D2 16	A#1 16	C2 16	A1 8	C2 8.
A#1 8.	A1 8	A1 8	C2 32	D2 8	C2 8	A#1 16	A1 16	A#1 16
C2 16	A1 16	A#1 16	G1 8

CHORI CHORI CHUPKE CHUPKE
[MEHANDI MEHANDI]

Music by Anu Malik. Lyrics by Sameer

© Copyright 2000 Universal Music India Limited. Universal Music Publishing Limited, Elsinore House, 77 Fulham Palace Road, London W6 8JA. All Rights Reserved. International Copyright Secured.

E1 4	E1 16	E1 16	E1 16	E1 16			TEMPO 100
F1 16	E1 16	E1 16	F1 16	E1 16	E1 16	F1 16	E1 16	A1 16
F1 16	F1 8	A1 16	F1 16	F1 8	E1 16	D1 8	E1 16	D1 8
E1 16	D1 16	E1 16	E1 16	E1 16	F1 16	G#1 16	F1 16	G#1 16
A1 16	B1 4	B1 8	B1 8	D2 8	D2 16	D2 8	D2 16	A1 16
A1 16	G#1 16	A1 16	G#1 16	A1 16	G#1 16	F1 16	E1 16	D1 16

ASIF ALI KHAN
[MEIN TENU VAIKHI JAWAAN]

Traditional
Arranged by Asif Ali Khan

© Copyright 2002 Copyright Control.
All Rights Reserved. International Copyright Secured.

C2 4	C2 4	C2 8	A#1 8	G#1 8			TEMPO 225
G1 8	A#1 4	A#1 4	A#1 8	G#1 8	G1 8	F1 8	G#1 4	G#1 4
G#1 8	G1 8	F1 8	D#1 8	G1 2	C1 4	D#1 4	D#1 4	F1 4
F1 4	G1 4	G1 4	G#1 4	G1 4	C1 4	D#1 4	F1 4	F1 8
G1 8	G#1 8	G1 8	F1 2				

HUM APPKE HAIN KOUN
[PEHLA PEHLAR PYAR]
Music by Raam-Laxman. Lyrics by Dev Kohli

© Copyright 1994 Saregama India Limited.Saregama PLC,
Unit 3, Bush Industrial Estate, Standard Road, Park Royal, London NW10 6HD.
All Rights Reserved. International Copyright Secured.

F3 16	D#3 32	D3 32	C#3 32	C3 32			TEMPO 125
B2 32	A#2 32	A2 32	G#2 32	G2 32	F2 32	E2 16	F2 4	- 8
E2 16	F2 16	G2 16	G#2 16	G2 16	F2 16	G2 16	G#2 16	G2 16
F2 16	G2 8	G2 16	G2 8	G2 16	F2 16	F2 16	G2 16	G#2 16
G2 16	F2 16	G2 16	G#2 16	G2 16	F2 16	F2 8	F2 16	F2 8
D3 32	E3 32	F3 16					

DILWALE DULHANIA LE JAYENGE
[TUJHE DEKHA TO]
Music by Jatin-Lalit. Lyrics by Anand Bakshi

© Copyright 1995 Saregama India Limited.Saregama PLC,
Unit 3, Bush Industrial Estate, Standard Road, Park Royal, London NW10 6HD.
All Rights Reserved. International Copyright Secured.

B1 16	C2 16	B1 16	A1 16	B1 2.			TEMPO 112
B1 16	C2 16	B1 16	A1 16	B1 2.	C2 16	D2 16	C2 16	B1 16
C2 32	D2 32	C2 2	C2 8	E2 8	E2 8	F2 32	E2 32.	D2 4.
- 8	B1 16	C2 16	D2 16	E2 16	G2 16	F#2 16	E2 8	F#2 16
E2 16	D2 8.	B1 16	C2 16	D2 16	E2 16	C2 16	D2 16	B1 4

AM TO PM

Words & Music by Christina Milian, Christian Karlsson & Pontus Winnberg

© Copyright 2001 Murlyn Songs AB, Sweden/Havana Brown Publishing/Songs Of Universal Incorporated, USA. Universal Music Publishing Limited, Elsinore House, 77 Fulham Palace Road, London W6 8JA. All Rights Reserved. International Copyright Secured.

C2 8	C2 16	C2 16	C2 8	A#1 8			TEMPO 100
C2 4	- 8	- 16	C2 16	C2 16	C2 16	C2 16	C2 8
A#1 8	C2 4	- 4	C2 16	C2 16	C2 16	C2 16	D2 8
A#1 4	- 8	- 16	A#1 16	A#1 16	A#1 8	A#1 16	C2 8	C2 16
- 16	C1 8	D#1 16	C1 8.	D#1 16	C1 16	G1 8	A#1 16	G1 8.
A#1 16	G1 16	C1 8	D#1 16	C1 8.

BABY COME ON OVER

Words & Music by Anders Bagge, Arnthor Birgisson & Samantha Mumba

© Copyright 2000 Murlyn Songs/Universal Music Publishing Limited, Elsinore House, 77 Fulham Palace Road, London W6 8JA (40%)/Chrysalis Music Limited, The Chrysalis Building, Bramley Road, London W10 6SP (40%)/Warner/Chappell Music Limited, Griffin House, 161 Hammersmith Road, London W6 8BS (20%). All Rights Reserved. International Copyright Secured.

C2 8	A#1 8	A1 8	G1 8	A1 8	A1 8	- 16	TEMPO 100
G1 8	F1 8	- 4	D1 16	D1 16	A#1 8	A#1 8	
- 16	F1 8	E1 8	- 8	- 16	C2 8		
A#1 8	A1 8	A1 8	- 16	E1 8	D1 8		
- 4	C1 16	D1 8	G1 8	A1 8	G1 8		

FLY BY II

Words & Music by Mikkel SE, Hallgeir Rustan, Tor Erik Hermansen, Simon Webbe, Randy Alpert & Herb Alpert

© Copyright 2001 Almo Music Corporation/Rondor Music (London) Limited (50%)/EMI Music Publishing Limited (30%)/Sony/ATV Music Publishing (UK) Limited (15%)/Universal Music Publishing Limited (5%).
All Rights Reserved. International Copyright Secured.

D2 16	D2 16	D2 8	D2 16	A1 16	C2 16	- 16	TEMPO 100
D2 4	- 4	D2 16	D2 16	D2 16	D2 16	D2 16	A1 16	C2 16
- 16	D2 4	- 4	G2 8	G2 8	G2 16	A2 16	G2 16	F2 16
F2 4	- 4	G2 8	G2 8
G2 16	A2 16	G2 16	F2 16
F2 4	D2 8	D2 4

HELLA GOOD

Words & Music by Gwen Stefani, Chad Hugo, Pharrell Williams & Tony Kanal

© Copyright 2002 World Of The Dolphin Music/Chase Chad Music/Waters Of Nazareth Publishing, USA. Universal/MCA Music Limited, Elsinore House, 77 Fulham Palace Road, London W6 8JA (50%)/EMI Music Publishing Limited, 127 Charing Cross Road, London WC2H 0QY (50%). All Rights Reserved. International Copyright Secured.

G2 16	G2 16	G1 16	G1 16	G2 16		TEMPO 112
G2 16	G#2 4	- 4	- 8	G#2 16	G#2 16	G#1 16	G#1 16	G#2 16
G#2 16	G1 16	- 8	- 16	G2 16	G1 16	G1 16	G2 16	G2 16
G1 16	G1 16	G2 16	G2 16	G#2 4	- 1	- 16	F2 16	F2 16
F2 16	G2 8	F2 8	G2 8	F2 16	G2 8	- 16	F2 8	G2 8
F2 8	A2 4	F2 8	D2 4	D2 4

IN YOUR WORLD

Lyrics & Music by Matthew Bellamy

© Copyright 2002 Taste Music Limited, 1 Prince Of Wales Passage,
117 Hampstead Road, London NW1 3EF.
All Rights Reserved. International Copyright Secured.

A1 16	E2 16	D2 16	E2 16	C2 16			TEMPO 112
E2 16	B1 16	E2 16	A1 16	E2 16	G#1 16	E2 16	A1 16	E2 16
B1 16	E2 16	A1 16	E2 16	D2 16	E2 16	C2 16	E2 16	B1 16
E2 16	A1 16	E2 16	G#1 16	E2 16	A1 16	E2 16	B1 16	E2 16
A1 16	E2 16	G#1 16	E2 16	A1 16	E2 16	B1 16	E2 16	C2 16
E2 16	D2 16	E2 16	C2 16	E2 16	B1 16	E2 16	A1 8

JUST A DAY

Words & Music by Grant Nicholas

© Copyright 2001 Universal Music Publishing Limited, Elsinore House,
77 Fulham Palace Road, London W6 8JA.
All Rights Reserved. International Copyright Secured.

F#2 8	- 8	F#2 8	E2 8	- 8			TEMPO 180
E2 4.	F#2 8	- 8	F#2 8	E2 8	- 8	B1 4.	F#2 8	- 8
F#2 8	E2 8	- 8	E2 4.	G#2 8	- 8	F#2 8	E2 8	- 8
C#2 4.	F#2 8	- 8	F#2 8	E2 8	- 8	E2 4.	F#2 8	- 8
F#2 8	E2 8	- 8	B1 4.	F#2 8	- 8	F#2 8	E2 8	- 8
E2 4.	G#2 8	- 8	F#2 8	E2 8	- 8	C#2 4.

KISS KISS
Words & Music by Aksu Sezen, Juliette Jaimes & Steve Welton-Jaimes

© Copyright 2001 Universal Music Publishing Limited, Elsinore House, 77 Fulham Palace Road, London W6 8JA.
All Rights Reserved. International Copyright Secured.

G1 8	A1 8	A1 8	E1 8	G1 8				TEMPO 180
A1 8	A1 8	- 8	G1 8	A1 8	B1 8	C2 8	B1 32	C2 32
B1 16	A1 8	A1 8	G1 8	G1 8	A1 8	A1 8	E1 8	G1 8
A1 8	A1 8	- 8	G1 8	A1 8	B1 8	C2 8	B1 32	C2 32
B1 16	A1 8	A1 8	G1 8	A1 8	- 8	A1 8	E1 8	G1 8
A1 8	A1 8							

LAZY
Words & Music by David Byrne, Darren Rock, Ashley Beedle & Darren House

© Copyright 2002 Moldy Fig Music/Warner/Chappell Music Limited (50%)/Deconstruction Songs Limited/BMG Music Publishing Limited (33.33%)/Chrysalis Music Limited (16.67%).
All Rights Reserved. International Copyright Secured.

D#2 1	D#2 2	D#2 8	D2 8	C2 8				TEMPO 180
A#1 8	C2 2.	F1 1	- 8	D#2 1	F2 2	D#2 8	D2 8	C2 8
A#1 8	C2 2.	F1 1	- 4	D#2 1	D#2 2	D#2 8	D2 8	C2 8
A#1 8	C2 2.	F1 1	- 8	F2 2	D#2 8	D2 8	C2 8	A#1 8
C2 2.	F1 1							

LIGHT MY FIRE

Words & Music by Jim Morrison, Robbie Krieger,
Ray Manzarek & John Densmore

© Copyright 1967 Doors Music Company, USA. Rondor Music (London) Limited, 10A Parsons Green, London SW6 4TW for the United Kingdom and the Republic of Ireland. All Rights Reserved. International Copyright Secured.

G#1 8	B1 8	G#1 8	B1 8	G#1 8			TEMPO 112
B1 8	A#1 4	G#1 2	- 4	- 8	- 16	G#1 8	B1 8	G#1 8
B1 8	G#1 8	B1 4	A#1 8	G#1 4	G#1 4	- 2	- 16	B1 8
G#1 8	B1 8	G#1 8	B1 4	F#1 8	G#1 4	- 2	- 16	B1 4
G#1 8	B1 8	G#1 8	B1 4	A#1 4	G#1 4	- 2	- 8	- 16
F#1 8	F#1 8	F#1 8	F#1 8	F1 8	F1 4	C#1 2		

A LITTLE LESS CONVERSATION

Words & Music by Billy Strange & Scott Davis

© Copyright 1968 Gladys Music Incorporated, USA. Carlin Music Corporation, Iron Bridge House, 3 Bridge Approach, London NW1 8BD for the British Commonwealth (excluding Canada and Australasia) the Republic of Ireland, Greece and Israel. All Rights Reserved. International Copyright Secured.

D2 8	D2 8	E2 4	E2 4	E2 8			TEMPO 225
G2 4	G2 4	B1 8	D2 8	D2 8	E2 4	E2 4	D2 4	- 2
- 8	B1 8	D2 4	E2 4	E2 4	E2 8	G2 4	G2 8	G2 8
- 8	- 4	B1 8	C#2 8	C#2 8	E2 4	E2 4	E2 8	G2 4
G2 4	G2 8	- 4	G2 8	E2 8	G2 8	E2 8	E2 8	E2 8
G2 4.	B1 4	B1 8	B1 8	B1 8	C#2 8	E2 4	G2 4	E2 4.

ONE NIGHT STAND

Words & Music by Mikkel SE, Hallgeir Rustan, Tor Erik Hermansen,
Alesha Dixon, Sabrina Washington & Su-Elise Nash

© Copyright 2001 Universal Music Publishing Limited (50%)/EMI Music Publishing
Limited (33.33%)/Sony/ATV Music Publishing (UK) Limited (16.67%).
All Rights Reserved. International Copyright Secured.

| - | A1 | D2 | F2 | E2 | | | TEMPO |
| 8 | 8 | 8 | 8 | 8 | | | 112 |

| C2 | G1 | A1 | - | A1 | D2 | F2 | E2 | C2 |
| 8 | 8 | 8 | 8 | 8 | 8 | 8 | 8 | 8 |

| G1 | A1 | - | A1 | D2 | F2 | E2 | C2 | G1 |
| 8 | 8 | 8 | 8 | 8 | 8 | 8 | 8 | 8 |

| A1 | - | G1 | F1 | E1 | - | A1 | D2 | F2 |
| 8 | 4 | 4 | 4 | 4 | 8 | 8 | 8 | 8 |

| E2 | C2 | G1 | A1 | - | A1 | D2 | F2 | E2 |
| 8 | 8 | 8 | 8 | 8 | 8 | 8 | 8 | 8 |

| C2 | G1 | A1 |
| 8 | 8 | 8 |

ONE STEP CLOSER

Words & Music by Cathy Dennis, Mike Percy & Tim Lever

© Copyright 2002 19 Music Limited/BMG Music Publishing Limited, Bedford House,
69-79 Fulham High Street, London SW6 3JW (66.67%)/EMI Music Publishing Limited,
127 Charing Cross Road, London WC2H 0QY (33.33%).
All Rights Reserved. International Copyright Secured.

| G2 | E2 | C2 | C2 | G2 | | | TEMPO |
| 4 | 4 | 8 | 8 | 8 | | | 125 |

| F#2 | D2 | B1 | C2 | D2 | F#2 | F#2 | G2 | F#2 |
| 4 | 4 | 4 | 8 | 4 | 4 | 8 | 8 | 8 |

| E2 | E2 | D2 | B1 | - | E2 | F#2 | G2 | G2 |
| 8 | 8. | 16 | 4 | 8 | 4 | 4 | 4 | 4 |

| A2 | G2 | G2 | G2 | F#2 | F#2 | - | E2 | D2 |
| 8 | 8 | 8 | 8 | 8 | 8 | 16 | 8 | 8 |

| D2 | - | D2 | - | F#2 | E2 | F#2 | - | F#2 |
| 16 | 16 | 8 | 8 | 8 | 8 | 8 | 8 | 8 |

| E2 | F#2 | E2 | G2 | F#2 | E2 |
| 8 | 8 | 8 | 8 | 4 | 4 |

OVERPROTECTED

Words & Music by Max Martin & Rami

© Copyright 2001 Maratone/Zomba Music Publishers Limited,
165-167 High Road, London NW10 2SG.
All Rights Reserved. International Copyright Secured.

C1 16	C1 16	C1 16	D1 16	D1 8.			TEMPO 90
D1 16	- 16	D1 16	D#1 16	D#1 8	- 1	- 8	C1 16	C1 16
C1 16	D1 16	D1 16	- 16	D1 16	D1 16	D1 16	D#1 16	D#1 8
- 1	- 8	D#1 8	F1 8	F1 16	- 16	F1 16	F1 8	F1 16
G1 16	G1 8	- 4	F1 16	G1 16	G#1 16	G1 16	F1 16	- 16
D#1 8.	F1 8.	G1 16	F1 4	- 8	D#1 16	D1 16	- 16	C1 4

RAPTURE

Words & Music by Markus Moser & Nadia Ali

© Copyright 2001 Renemade Music/EMI Music Publishing Limited,
127 Charing Cross Road, London WC2H 0QY.
All Rights Reserved. International Copyright Secured.

D#2 8	F2 4	A#1 8	A#1 8	C2 8			TEMPO 125
C#2 8	D#2 8	D#2 8	F2 4	A#1 8	A#1 8	C2 8	C#2 8	D#2 8
D#2 8	F2 2	- 1	- 4	D#2 8	F2 4	A#1 8	A#1 8	C2 8
C#2 8	D#2 8	D#2 8	F2 4	A#1 8	A#1 8	C2 8	C#2 8	G#2 8
F2 2							

SHOULDA WOULDA COULDA

Words & Music by Beverley Knight & Craig Wiseman

© Copyright 2002 Minaret Music Limited, 59 Glenthorne Road, London W6 OLJ (50%)/
Rondor Music (London) Limited, 1OA Parsons Green, London SW6 4TW (50%).
All Rights Reserved. International Copyright Secured.

F#2 8	A2 8	A2 16	F#2 8	E2 16			TEMPO 70
D2 4	B2 16	A2 16	A2 16	F#2 16	E2 16	D2 16	F#2 8	E2 4
E2 16	F#2 32	E2 32	D2 16	E2 16	D2 4	- 8	B1 16	D2 16
D2 16	B1 .16	D2 16	B1 16	D2 16	B1 16	D2 16	E2 16	D2 32
E2 8	- 4	B1 16	D2 16	D2 16	B1 16	D2 16	B1 16	D2 8
G2 8	F#2 16	E2 8.					

SUNGLASSES AT NIGHT

Words & Music by Corey Hart

© Copyright 1992 Harco Productions Limited/Liesse Publishing, USA. Warner/Chappell
Music Limited, Griffin House, 161 Hammersmith Road, London W6 8BS (75%)/
Copyright Control (25%).
All Rights Reserved. International Copyright Secured.

A1 8	A1 8	F2 8	F2 8	E2 8			TEMPO 140
E2 8	D2 8	D2 8	A1 8	A1 8	F2 8	F2 8	E2 8	E2 8
D2 8	D2 8	B1 8	B1 8	F2 8	F2 8	E2 8	E2 8	D2 8
D2 8	B1 8	B1 8	F2 8	F2 8	E2 8	E2 8	D2 8	D2 8
A#1 8	A#1 8	F2 8	F2 8	E2 8	E2 8	D2 8	D2 8	C2 8
C2 8	F2 8	F2 8	E2 8	E2 8	D2 8	D2 8		

ALL I WANT

Words & Music by David Brant, Alan Glass, Maryanne Morgan & Alesha Dixon

© Copyright 2001 Reverb Music Limited, Reverb House, Bennett Street, London W4 2AH (63.33%)/Peoplesound.com Limited/EMI Music Publishing Limited, 127 Charing Cross Road, London WC2H 0QY (31.67%)/ Universal Music Publishing Limited, Elsinore House, 77 Fulham Palace Road, London W6 8JA (5%).
All Rights Reserved. International Copyright Secured.

						TEMPO
A2 4	A2 8	G2 8	- 8	- 4		125
G2 8	F2 16	G2 8	G2 8	A2 16	- 8	D2 8	F2 8	G2 8
A2 4	A2 8	G2 8	- 4	- 16	F2 16	G2 8	F2 16	G2 8
G2 8	- 8	- 16	F2 8	G2 8	A2 4	A2 8		
- 16	G2 16	G2 16	G2 8	G2 16	G2 16	G2 8	F2 16	
G2 8	A2 8	- 16	A1 8	A1 8	A1 8	A1 8	A2 2	G2 2

BAD BABYSITTER

Words & Music by Concetta Kirschner, Erik Meltzer & Milo Berger

© Copyright 2002 Universal Music Publishing Limited, Elsinore House, 77 Fulham Palace Road, London W6 8JA (66.67%)/SMV 5-7 Publishing GmbH/Bucks Music Limited, Onward House, 11 Uxbridge Street, London W8 7TQ (30%)/Copyright Control (3.33%).
All Rights Reserved. International Copyright Secured.

					TEMPO
F1 8	G1 16	- 8	F1 8	G1 16	80
A#1 32	D2 16	- 16	D#1 8	- 8	C2 8	- 8	A1 16	D2 16
- 8	F1 8	- 8	D2 8	- 8	F1 8	G1 16	- 8	F1 8
G1 16	A#1 32	D2 16	- 16	D#1 8	- 8	C2 8	- 8	A1 16
D2 16	- 8	F1 8	- 8	D2 8	- 8	F1 8	G1 16	

BOOTYLICIOUS

Words & Music by Beyoncé Knowles, Robert Fusari, Falonte Moore & Stevie Nicks

© Copyright 2001 Beyoncé Publishing/Sony/ATV Tunes LLC/June-Bug Alley/Lonte Music/
Welsh Witch Music/Sony/ATV Songs LLC, USA. Sony/ATV Music Publishing (UK) Limited
(87.5%)/EMI Songs Limited (12.5%).
All Rights Reserved. International Copyright Secured.

E1 **8**	E1 **16**	E1 **16**	G1 **16**	F#1 **8**				**TEMPO 100**
E1 **16**	E1 **8**	G1 **8**	F#1 **8**	E1 **8**	E1 **8**	E1 **16**	E1 **16**	G1 **16**
F#1 **8**	E1 **16**	E1 **8**	A1 **8**	F#1 **8**	E1 **8**	E1 **8**	E1 **16**	E1 **16**
G1 **16**	F#1 **8**	E1 **16**	E1 **8**	G1 **8**	D1 **8**	E1 **8**	A1 **8**	A1 **16**
A1 **8**	A1 **8**	B1 **16**	G1 **8**	E1 **8**	D1 **8**	D1 **16**	E1 **8**	

EYE KNOW

Words & Music by Paul Huston, Kelvin Mercer, Vincent Mason, David Jolicoeur, Walter Becker & Donald Fagen

© Copyright 1989 Tee Girl Music Publishing/Duchess Music Corporation, USA. IQ Music
Limited, Commercial House, 52 Perrymount Road, Haywards Heath, West Sussex RH16 3DT
(50%)/Universal/MCA Music Limited, Elsinore House, 77 Fulham Palace Road,
London W6 8JA (50%). All Rights Reserved. International Copyright Secured.

G#1 **8**	- **8**	G#1 **8**	A#1 **16**	C2 **16**				**TEMPO 125**
- **4**	- **8**	D#2 **16**	- **16**	G#1 **8**	- **8**	G#1 **8**	A#1 **16**	C2 **16**
- **2**	G#1 **8**	- **8**	G#1 **8**	A#1 **16**	C2 **16**	- **4**	- **8**	D#2 **16**
- **16**	G#1 **8**	- **8**	G#1 **8**	A#1 **16**	C2 **16**	- **2**	- **8**	C2 **8**
C2 **8**	C2 **8**	D#2 **8**	- **8**	D#2 **8**	- **8**	G#1 **8**	- **8**	G#1 **8**
A#1 **16**	C2 **4**							

FAMILY AFFAIR

Words & Music by Mary J. Blige, Bruce Miller, Andre Young, Camara Kambon, Mike Elizondo, Melvin Bradford, Asiah Louis & Luchana Lodge

© Copyright 2001 Universal/MCA Music Limited (30%)/Warner/Chappell Music Limited (22%)/Windswept Music (London) Limited (14%)/Copyright Control (34%). All Rights Reserved. International Copyright Secured.

G3 **4**	G2 **4**	G2 **4**	G2 **4**	G2 **4**				TEMPO **225**
D2 **4**	F2 **4**	G2 **4**	G2 **4**	D2 **4**	F2 **4**	G2 **8**	G2 **8**	A2 **8**
A#2 **4**	A2 **4**	G2 **4**	A2 **4**	D2 **4**	D2 **4**	D2 **4**	D2 **4**	A1 **4**
C2 **4**	D2 **4**	D2 **4**	A1 **4**	C2 **4**	D2 **4**	D2 **4**	F2 **4**	A2 **4**
F2 **4**	G2 **4**							

FREAK LIKE ME

Words & Music by Gary Numan, Eugene Hanes, Marc Valentine, Loren Hill, William Collins, George Clinton & Gary Cooper

© Copyright 2002 Beggars Banquet Music Limited/Universal/Momentum Music Limited (50%)/Rubber Band Music Incorporated/Universal Music Publishing Limited (25%)/Hanes Hill & Valentine Music/Notting Hill Music (UK) Limited (25%). All Rights Reserved. International Copyright Secured.

D2 **16**	C#2 **16**	B1 **8**	A1 **8**	F#1 **8**				TEMPO **125**
E1 **8**	D1 **8**	D#1 **8**	- **8**	E1 **8**	G1 **8**	B1 **8**	- **8**	E1 **8**
A1 **8**	C#2 **8**	- **8**	D2 **16**	C#2 **16**	B1 **8**	A1 **8**	F#1 **8**	E1 **8**
D1 **8**	D#1 **8**	- **8**	E1 **8**	G1 **8**	B1 **8**	- **8**	E1 **8**	A1 **8**
C#2 **8**	- **8**	F#2 **16**	E2 **16**	D2 **8**	C#2 **8**	B1 **8**	A1 **8**	F#1 **8**
E1 **8**	- **8**	E1 **8**	G1 **8**	B1 **8**	- **8**	E1 **8**	A1 **8**	C#2 **8**

I GOT 5 ON IT

*Words & Music by G. Husbands, J. Ellis Jr., A. Gilmour, J. King,
D.Foster, T. McElroy, R. Bell, C. Smith, R. Mickens, D.Boyce,
R. Westfield, D. Thomas, R. Bell & G. Brown*

© Copyright 1995 EMI Music Publishing Limited (63.33%)/Global Chrysalis Music Publishing Company Limited (16.67%)/The International Music Network Limited (10%)/EMI Music Publishing (WP) Limited (10%). All Rights Reserved. International Copyright Secured

A#1 8	C#3 8	F2 8	C3 8	D#2 4.			TEMPO 90
-16	F1 16	A#1 8	C#3 8	F2 8	C3 2	-16	F1 16	A#1 8
C#3 8	F2 8	C3 8	D#2 4.	-16	F1 16	A#1 8	C#3 8	F2 8
C3 4	G#2 8	F2 8	A#2 8	F#1 8	A#2 8	C#2 8	G#2 8	C2 4.
-16	C#1 16	F#1 8	A#2 8	C#2 8	G#2 4	G#1 8	A1 4	A#1 8
A#1 8								

IT TAKES MORE

*Words by Ms Dynamite
Music by Punch*

© Copyright 2002 EMI Music Publishing Limited, 127 Charing Cross Road, London WC2H 0QY (50%)/Copyright Control (50%).
All Rights Reserved. International Copyright Secured.

D2 8	E2 8	F2 8.	E2 16	D2 4			TEMPO 90
-4	F2 8.	F2 16	E2 8.	D2 16	C2 8	D2 8	E2 8	-8
C2 8	C2 8	D2 8.	C2 16	B1 4	-4	A1 8	-16	A1 16
C2 8	-16	A1 16	C2 16	-16	A1 16	-16	A1 8	

MS JACKSON

Words & Music by Antwan Patton, Andre Benjamin & David Sheats

© Copyright 2001 Gnat Booty Music/Dungeon Rat Music, USA.
Chrysalis Music Limited, The Chrysalis Building, Bramley Road, London W10 6SP (83.33%)/
EMI Music Publishing Limited, 127 Charing Cross Road, London WC2H 0QY (16.67%).
All Rights Reserved. International Copyright Secured.

A1 8	E2 8	D2 8	E2 8	D2 8				TEMPO 90
E2 16	D2 8	E2 16	A1 16	- 16	A1 8	E2 8	D2 8	E2 8
D2 8	E2 16	D2 8	E2 16	A1 8	- 8	- 16	A1 16	E2 16
D2 16	C2 16	D2 8	E2 16	- 4	- 8	E2 8	E2 8	E2 8
G2 8.	F2 16	E2 8						

ORGAN DONOR

By Josh Davis

© Copyright 1996 Mowax Music, USA. Universal/MCA Music Limited,
Elsinore House, 77 Fulham Palace Road, London W6 8JA.
All Rights Reserved. International Copyright Secured.

G#1 8	F#1 8	G#1 8	E1 8	F#1 8				TEMPO 100
D#1 8	E1 8	C#1 8	G#1 8	F#1 8	G#1 8	E1 8	F#1 8	D#1 8
E1 8	C#1 16	E1 16	C#1 16	D#1 16	E1 16	F#1 16	D#1 16	E1 16
F#1 16	G#1 16	E1 16	F#1 16	G#1 16	G#1 16	F#1 16	C#1 16	G#1 16
E1 16	C#1 16	D#1 16	E1 16	F#1 16	D#1 16	E1 16	F#1 16	G#1 16
E1 16	F#1 16	G#1 16	G#1 16	F#1 16	C#1 16	G#1 16	C#1 16	

PERFECT GENTLEMAN
Words & Music by Wyclef Jean, Jerry Duplessis & Hope Harris

© Copyright 2000 Sony/ATV Music Publishing (UK) Limited (45%)/EMI Music Publishing Limited (45%)/Notting Hill Music (UK) Limited (10%). All Rights Reserved. International Copyright Secured.

| E2 | C2 | G1 | C2 | E2 | | | TEMPO |
| 8 | 8 | 8 | 8 | 8 | | | 125 |

| C2 | G1 | C2 | D2 | B1 | G1 | B1 | D2 | B1 |
| 8 | 8 | 8 | 8 | 8 | 8 | 8 | 8 | 8 |

| G1 | B1 | C2 | A1 | F1 | A1 | D2 | B1 | G1 |
| 8 | 8 | 8 | 8 | 8 | 8 | 8 | 8 | 8 |

| B1 | - | E2 | E2 | E2 | E2 | D2 | C2 | C2 |
| 8 | 8 | 8 | 8 | 8 | 8 | 16 | 8 | 8 |

| - | D2 | D2 | D2 | D2 | C2 | B1 | B1 | - |
| 8 | 8 | 8 | 8 | 8 | 16 | 8 | 8 | 8 |

| C2 | C2 | C2 | C2 | C2 | D2 | C2 |
| 8 | 8 | 8 | 8 | 16 | 8 | 8 |

PURPLE PILLS
Words & Music by Von Carlisle, DeShaun Holton, Rufus Johnson, Marshall Mathers, Ondre Moore, Denaun Porter & Jeffrey Bass

© Copyright 2001 EMI Music Publishing Limited, 127 Charing Cross Road, London WC2H 0QY (31.36%)/EMI Songs Limited, 127 Charing Cross Road, London WC2H 0QY (7.84%)/Copyright Control (19.96%). All Rights Reserved. International Copyright Secured.

| G#1 | D#2 | - | - | D#2 | | | TEMPO |
| 4 | 4 | 4 | 8 | 8 | | | 125 |

| C#2 | B1 | C#2 | - | C#2 | B1 | A#1 | B1 | - |
| 8 | 8 | 8 | 2 | 8 | 8 | 8 | 8 | 2 |

| G#1 | A#1 | G#1 | F#1 | - | - | B1 | B1 | G#1 |
| 8 | 8 | 8 | 8 | 2 | 4 | 8 | 8 | 8 |

| G#1 | F#1 | G#1 | A#1 | - | B1 | B1 | G#1 | G#1 |
| 8 | 8 | 8 | 8 | 8 | 8 | 8 | 8 | 8 |

| F#1 | G#1 | A#1 | - | B1 | B1 | G#1 | G#1 | F#1 |
| 8 | 8 | 8 | 8 | 8 | 8 | 8 | 8 | 8 |

| G#1 | A#1 | B1 | G#1 | B1 | G#1 | B1 | B1 | G#1 |
| 8 | 8 | 8 | 8 | 8 | 8 | 8. | 8. | 8. |

PUSH IT

Words & Music by Hurby Azor & Ray Davies

© Copyright 1987 Next Plateau Music Incorporated/Warner/Chappell Music Limited,
Griffin House, 161 Hammersmith Road, London W6 8BS (98%)/Edward Kassner Music
Company Limited, Units 6 & 7, 11 Wyfold Road, London SW6 6SE (2%).
All Rights Reserved. International Copyright Secured.

A1 8	- 8	E1 8	A1 8	- 8		TEMPO 125
E1 8	- 8	G1 8	- 8	E1 8	G1 8	E1 8	B1 8	C2 8
B1 4	A1 8	- 8	E1 8	A1 8	- 8	E1 8	- 8	G1 8
- 1	A1 8	- 8	E2 8	D2 8	- 8	C2 8	- 8	B1 8
- 8	G1 8	- 8	G1 8	B1 8	C2 8	B1 8	G1 8	A1 8
- 8	E2 8	D2 8	- 8	C2 8	- 8	B1 8	- 8	G1 8

WHITE LINES (DON'T DO IT)

Words & Music by Sylvia Robinson & Melvin Glover

© Copyright 1983 Gambi Music Incorporated, USA. IQ Music Limited, Commercial
House, 52 Perrymount Road, Haywards Heath, West Sussex RH16 3DT.
All Rights Reserved. International Copyright Secured.

G2 16	- 16	G2 16	F2 16	- 16		TEMPO 112
D2 16	F2 16	D2 16	F2 16	G2 16	- 16	F2 16	- 16	D2 16
F2 16	G2 16	G2 16	- 16	G2 16	F2 16	- 16	D2 16	F2 16
D2 16	G2 16	F2 16	D2 16	C#2 16	C2 16	A#1 16	G1 16	F1 16

WHO'S THAT GIRL?

Words & Music by Eve Jeffers, Sheldon Harris,
Darrin Dean & Ignatius Jackson

© Copyright 2001 Blondie Rockwell/Teflon Hitz/Icepickjay Publishing/Dead Game
Publishing/Ryde Or Die Publishing, USA. Universal Music Publishing Limited, Elsinore
House, 77 Fulham Palace Road, London W6 8JA (35%)/Copyright Control (65%).
All Rights Reserved. International Copyright Secured.

| F#1 | - | - | - | F#1 | | TEMPO |
| 4 | 4 | 8 | 16 | 8 | | 200 |

| F#1 | F#1 | F#1 | F#1 | F#1 | - | F#1 | F1 | - |
| 8 | 4 | 8 | 4 | 8 | 8 | 8 | 2 | 4 |

| F1 | F#1 | - | D#2 | - | A#1 | D#2 | - | A#1 |
| 4 | 2 | 2 | 4 | 8 | 8 | 4 | 8 | 8 |

| D#2 | - | A#1 | D#2 | A#1 | D#2 | A#1 | D#2 | - |
| 4 | 8 | 8 | 8 | 8 | 8 | 8 | 4 | 8 |

| A#1 | A#1 | - | A#1 | C#2 | A#1 | A#1 | D#2 | A#1 |
| 4. | 2 | 2 | 4 | 4. | 4. | 4 | 4. | 4. |

| A#1 | D#2 |
| 4 | 2 |

WITHOUT ME

Words & Music by Marshall Mathers & Jeff Bass

© Copyright 2002 Eight Mile Style/Ensign Music Corporation/
Famous Music Corporation, USA.
All Rights Reserved. International Copyright Secured.

| D2 | A2 | A#2 | A2 | G2 | | TEMPO |
| 8 | 32 | 8 | 8 | 8 | | 125 |

| D2 | - | - | D2 | C2 | D2 | E2 | F2 | D2 |
| 8 | 4 | 8 | 8 | 8 | 8 | 32 | 8 | 8 |

| - | - | D2 | C2 | D2 | C2 |
| 4 | 8 | 8 | 8 | 8 | 8 |

| A#1 | - | - | A#1 | A1 | F1 |
| 8 | 4 | 8 | 8 | 8 | 8 |

| G1 |
| 4 |

CHASE THE SUN

Words & Music by Marco Baroni, Domenico Canu,
Sergio Della Monica, Simon Duffy & Alessandro Neri

© Copyright 2001 Bustin' Loose Music/Zomba Music Publishers Limited, 165-167 High Road, London NW10 2SG (54.16%)/Warner/Chappell Music Limited, Griffin House, 161 Hammersmith Road, London W6 8BS (45.84%). All Rights Reserved. International Copyright Secured.

A1 4	E2 4	A1 8	E2 4	A1 8				TEMPO 125
G2 4	A1 8	G2 4	A1 8	G2 4	A1 4	E2 8	E2 8	D2 8
C2 8	B1 2	B1 16	C2 16	B1 8	A1 8	G1 8	G1 4.	E1 8
G1 8	A1 8	B1 4	A1 1	- 4	E2 4	E2 8	D2 8	C2 8
B1 2	C2 8	B1 8	A1 8	G1 8	G1 4.	E1 8	G1 8	A1 8
B1 4	A1 2							

COME WITH US

Words & Music by Tom Rowlands & Ed Simons

© Copyright 2002 Universal/MCA Music Limited, Elsinore House, 77 Fulham Palace Road, London W6 8JA. All Rights Reserved. International Copyright Secured.

G1 16	F1 16	G1 16	C2 16	A#1 16				TEMPO 112
G1 16	A#1 16	D2 16	C2 16	G#1 16	C2 16	D#2 16	D2 16	A#1 16
D2 16	F2 16	D#2 16	C2 16	D#2 16	G2 16	F2 16	D2 16	F2 16
G#2 16	G2 16	D#2 16	G2 16	A#2 16	F2 16	C#2 16	C2 16	A#1 16
G1 16								

CRAZY LOVE

Words & Music by Matt Coleman & Elisabeth Troy Antwi

© Copyright 2000 BMG Music Publishing Limited, Bedford House, 69-79 Fulham High Street, London SW6 3JW (50%)/Rondor Music (London) Limited, 10A Parsons Green, London SW6 4TW (50%).
All Rights Reserved. International Copyright Secured.

A1 32	E2 32	A2 32	B2 8	C3 8			TEMPO 125
- 8	B2 8	- 8	G2 4	A2 8	- 8	E2 16	- 16	F2 16
- 16	A2 16	- 16	E3 16	- 16	- 2	A2 16	- 16	A2 16
- 16	A2 16	- 16	A2 16	- 16	B2 16	- 16	- 8	C3 16
- 16	- 4	- 8	G2 16	- 16	A2 16

DIGITAL LOVE

Words & Music by Thomas Bangalter, Guy-Manuel de Homem-Christo, Carlos Sosa & George Duke

© Copyright 2001 Zomba Music Publishers Limited, 165-167 High Road, London NW10 2SG (75%)/Mycenae Music Publishing Company/Carlin Music Corporation, Iron Bridge House, 3 Bridge Approach, London NW1 8BD (25%).
All Rights Reserved. International Copyright Secured.

D1 8	D1 8	- 8	C#1 8	- 8			TEMPO 125
F#1 8	- 8	D1 4	C#2 16	D2 4	F#2 16	G#2 16	A2 16	F#2 16
D2 16	F#2 16	G#2 16	F#2 8	D1 8	D1 8	- 8	C#1 8	- 8
F#1 8	- 8	D1 4	C#2 16	D2 16	F#2 4	G#2 16	A2 16	F#2 16
D2 16	F#2 16	G#2 16	F#2 4

FREAK LIKE ME

Words & Music by Eugene Hanes, Marc Valentine, Loren Hill, William 'Bootsy' Collins, George Clinton & Gary Cooper

© Copyright 2000 Rubber Band Music Incorporated/Universal Music Publishing Limited, Elsinore House, 77 Fulham Palace Road, London W6 8JA (50%)/Hanes Hill & Valentine Music/Notting Hill Music (UK) Limited, 8B Berkeley Gardens, London W8 4AP (50%). All Rights Reserved. International Copyright Secured.

A#1 16	C2 16	A#1 16	G2 16	- 16			TEMPO 90	
G2 16	F2 16	G2 8	F2 16	- 16	F2 16	- 16	F2 16	D#2 16
F2 8	D#2 8	- 32	A#2 32	G2 8	G2 8	G2 8	F2 8	A#1 16
C2 16	A#1 16	G2 16	- 16	G2 16	- 16	G2 16	F2 16	G2 16
F2 16	G2 16	F2 16	- 16	A#2 8	C3 32	A#2 16	G2 16	- 16
D#2 16	- 16	G2 8	G2 8	F2 16				

GOTTA GET THRU THIS

Words & Music by Daniel Bedingfield

© Copyright 2001 Reverb Music Limited, Reverb House, Bennett Street, London W4 2AH. All Rights Reserved. International Copyright Secured.

G2 4	- 4	D#2 4	- 8	A#2 4			TEMPO 125	
- 4	- 8	A#1 8	- 16	A1 8	- 16	G1 4	- 8	D2 8
D#2 4	- 8	A#1 8	- 2	- 8	D2 8	D2 16	D2 16	D2 8
D2 8	A#1 8	- 4	D2 8	D2 16	D2 16	D2 8	D2 8	D#2 8
- 4	D2 8	D2 16	D2 16	D2 8	D2 8	D2 16	D2 16	D2 8
A#1 16	- 16	D2 16	D2 16	D#2 8	D2 16	- 8	D2 8	C2 4

JACK YOUR BODY

Words & Music by Steve 'Silk' Hurley

© Copyright 1986 Last Song Incorporated/Silktone Songs Incorporated, USA.
The International Music Network Limited, Independent House, 54 Larkshall Road,
London E4 6PD (75%)/Campbell Connelly & Company Limited, 8/9 Frith Street,
London W1D 3JB (25%). All Rights Reserved. International Copyright Secured.

G#1 4	G#1 8.	D#2 8	D#2 16	D#2 8				TEMPO 112
F#2 8	G#2 8	G#1 4	G#1 8.	D#2 8	D#2 16	D#2 8	F#2 8	D#2 8
G#1 4	G#1 8.	D#2 8	D#2 16	D#2 8	F#2 8	G#2 8	G#1 4	G#1 8.
D#2 8	G#1 16	C#2 16	G#1 16	B1 16	G#1 16	C#2 16	G#1 16	D#1 4
D#1 8.	A#1 8	D#1 16	G#1 16	D#1 16	F#1 16	D#1 16	G#1 16	C#1 16
D#1 4	D#1 8	A#1 16	D#1 16	G#1 16	D#1 16	F#1 8.	C#1 8	

LES FLEUR

Words & Music by Charles Stepney

© Copyright 1969 Embassy Music Corporation, USA.
Campbell Connelly & Company Limited, 8/9 Frith Street, London W1D 3JB.
All Rights Reserved. International Copyright Secured.

D#2 16	D#2 16	D#2 16	D#2 8	F2 16				TEMPO 90
G2 16	G#2 8	G2 8	F2 8	D#2 16	C#2 16	A#1 16	C#2 8	C#2 16
A#1 16	C#2 16	D#2 16	F2 16	D#2 16	- 16	D#2 16	D#2 16	D#2 16
D#2 8	F2 16	G2 16	G#2 8	G2 8	F2 8	D#2 16	C#2 16	A#1 16
C#2 8	C#2 16	A#1 16	C#2 16	D#2 16	F2 16	D#2 2		

THE LOGICAL SONG

Words & Music by Roger Hodgson & Richard Davies

© Copyright 1979 Delicate Music/Almo Music Corporation, USA.
Rondor Music (London) Limited, 10A Parsons Green, London SW6 4TW
for the United Kingdom and the Republic of Ireland.
All Rights Reserved. International Copyright Secured.

B1 8	C#2 8	C#2 8	C#2 4	A1 8		**TEMPO 160**
A1 8	B1 8	C#2 8	C#2 8	C#2 4	B1 8	A1 8	G#1 4	- 4
B1 8	B1 8	A1 8	G#1 4	- 8	B1 8	B1 8	B1 8	A1 8
G#1 8	F#1 4	A1 8	G#1 8	F#1 4.	A1 8	A1 8	B1 8	B1 8
C#2 8	C#2 8	C#2 4	A1 8	A1 8	B1 8	C#2 8	C#2 8	G#2 4
B1 8	A1 8	G#2 1	B1 8	B1 8	A1 8	G#1 4.

MOTHER

Words & Music by Julian Jonah & Danny Harrison

© Copyright 2002 BMG Music Publishing Limited, Bedford House, 69-79 Fulham High
Street, London SW6 3JW (50%)/Bucks Music Limited, Onward House,
11 Uxbridge Street, London W8 7TQ (50%).
All Rights Reserved. International Copyright Secured.

G1 16	F1 16	G1 16	F1 16	A#1 16		**TEMPO 125**
F1 16	G1 16	F1 16	A#1 16	F1 16	G1 16	F1 16	A#1 16	F1 16
C2 16	F1 16	D2 16	F1 16	C2 16	F1 16	A#1 16	F1 16	G1 16
F1 16	G1 16	F1 16	G1 16	F1 16	G1 16	F1 16	D1 16	F1 16
G1 4

MOVIN' TOO FAST

Words & Music by Fabio Raponi, Orlando Johnson & Ingo Schwartz

© Copyright 1999 Altatensione/Rossiter Road Srl, Italy. Universal Music Publishing Limited, Elsinore House, 77 Fulham Palace Road, London W6 8JA.
All Rights Reserved. International Copyright Secured.

D2 4	- 8	A1 4	C#2 4	D2 4			TEMPO 125
A2 4	A1 4	C#2 4	D2 4	D2 8	- 4	A1 4	C#2 4	D2 4
B2 4	A1 8	C#2 4	D2 8	- 8	F#2 4	- 8	B1 8	D2 8
E2 8	F#2 8	F#2 8	- 4	B1 8	B1 8	D2 8	E2 8	F#2 8
F#2 8	- 4	B1 8	B1 8	D2 16	D2 16	E2 8	F#2 8	F#2 8
- 8	D2 8	D2 32	E2 4

PIANO LOCO

Words & Music by Joel Samuels & Michael Rose

© Copyright 1975 MPL Communications Limited, 1 Soho Square, London W1.
All Rights Reserved. International Copyright Secured.

F2 8	C#2 16	A#1 16	F2 16	F#2 16			TEMPO 125
- 16	F2 8	C2 8	D#2 16	F#2 8	F#2 8	F2 8	C#2 16	A#1 16
F2 16	F#2 16	- 16	F2 8	C2 8	D#2 16	F#2 8	F#2 8	F2 8
C#2 16	A#1 16	F2 16	F#1 16	- 16	F2 8	C2 8	D#2 16	F#2 8
F#2 8	F2 8	C#2 16	A#1 16	F2 16	F#2 16	- 16	F2 8	A#2 16
A#2 16	A#2 16	A#2 8	A#2 16

PLAYED A-LIVE [THE BONGO SONG]
By Morten Friis, Uffe Savery & Michael Parsberg

© Copyright 2000 Sony/ATV Music Publishing (UK) Limited, 10 Great Marlborough Street, London W1F 7LP (80%)/Re-Flex/EMI Music Publishing Limited, 127 Charing Cross Road, London WC2H 0QY (20%). All Rights Reserved. International Copyright Secured.

B1 8	B1 8	G#1 16	B1 8.	B1 8				TEMPO 125
B1 8	G#1 16	B1 8.	A#1 8	A#1 8	F#1 16	A#1 8.	A#1 8	A#1 8
F#1 16	A#1 8	C#2 16	F#1 8	F#1 8	D#1 16	F#1 8.	F#1 8	F#1 8
D#1 16	F#1 8.	G#1 8	E2 8	G#1 16	E2 8.	G#1 8	E2 8	G#1 16
D#2 8	C#2 16	B1 8						

READY STEADY GO
Words & Music by Paul Oakenfold & Andy Gray

© Copyright 2002 Universal Music Publishing Limited, Elsinore House, 77 Fulham Palace Road, London W6 8JA (50%)/Mute Song, Lawford House, 429 Harrow Road, London W10 4RE (50%). All Rights Reserved. International Copyright Secured.

C#1 8	C#1 8	C#1 8	D#1 4	C#1 8				TEMPO 125
E1 8	C#1 8	C#2 8	C#2 8	C#2 8	D#2 4	E2 4	- 8	C#1 8
C#1 8	C#1 8	D#1 8	C#1 8	E1 8	C#1 8	C#2 8	C#2 8	C#2 8
D#2 4	E2 4	- 8	G#2 4	F#2 8	G#2 8	F#2 8	D#2 8	- 8
D#2 4	D#2 8	E2 4	D#2 8	- 8	D#2 4	D#2 8	E2 4	D#2 8
- 8	D#2 4	D#2 8	E2 4	D#2 4				

SET YOU FREE
Words & Music by Michael Lewis, Dale Longworth & Kevin O'Toole

© Copyright 1994 All Boys Music Limited, 222-224 Borough High Street, London SE1 1JX.
All Rights Reserved. International Copyright Secured.

G#1 16	F#1 16	G#1 16	F#1 16	G#1 8			TEMPO 125
F#1 16	G#1 8	F#1 16	G#1 8	C#2 8	C#2 8	G#1 16	F#1 16	G#1 16
F#1 16	G#1 8	F#1 16	G#1 8	F#1 16	G#1 8	C2 8	D#2 8	C2 8
- 8	C2 4	C#2 32	C2 8	A#1 4	A#1 8	- 8	A#1 4.	C2 32
A#1 8	G#1 8	C2 8	D#2 8	C2 8	- 8	C2 4	C#2 32	C2 8
A#1 4	A#1 8	- 8	A#1 4.	C2 32	A#1 8	G#1 8	C2 8	D#2 8

WEAPON OF CHOICE
Words & Music by Norman Cook, William 'Bootsy' Collins & Ashley Slater

© Copyright 2000 Universal Music Publishing Limited, Elsinore House, 77 Fulham Palace Road, London W6 8JA (66.67%)/Edel Publishing Limited/Sony/ATV Music Publishing (UK) Limited, 10 Great Marlborough Street, London W1F 7LP (33.33%).
All Rights Reserved. International Copyright Secured.

G#1 16	G#1 16	G#1 16	G#1 16	B1 16			TEMPO 100
B1 16	B1 16	B1 16	C#2 16	C#2 16	C#2 16	C#2 16	D2 16	D2 16
D2 16	D2 16	D#2 8	F#2 16	C#2 32	D2 32	C#2 16	B1 16	G#1 16
F#1 16	G#2 16	F#2 16	D#2 16	C#2 32	D2 32	C#2 16	B1 16	G#1 16
F#1 16	G#1 16

ALIVE

Words by Eddie Vedder
Music by Stone Gossard

© Copyright 1991 Write Treatage Music/Innocent Bystander, USA.
Universal Music Publishing Limited, Elsinore House, 77 Fulham Palace Road, London
W6 8JA (50%)/Sony/ATV Music Publishing (UK) Limited, 10 Great Marlborough Street,
London W1F 7LP (50%). All Rights Reserved. International Copyright Secured.

D#2 8	G#2 8	A#1 2	D#2 8	A#2 8	C3 2		TEMPO 140
A#2 2	D#2 8	G#2 8	A#1 2	D#2 8	A#2 8	C3 4.	A#2 8	C3 8
C#3 8	C3 8	A#2 8	G#2 4	A#1 2	D#2 8	A#2 2	C3 2	A#2 2
D#2 8	G#2 8	A#1 2	D#2 8	A#2 8	C3 4.	A#2 8	C3 8	C#3 8
C3 8	A#2 8	G#2 4						

ALL ALONG THE WATCHTOWER

Words & Music by Bob Dylan

© Copyright 1968 Dwarf Music, USA.
This arrangement © Copyright 2002 Dwarf Music.
All Rights Reserved. International Copyright Secured.

D#1 16	D#1 16	D#1 16	D#1 16	F1 16			TEMPO 112
F1 16	F1 16	F1 16	F1 16	G1 16	G1 16	G1 16	G1 16	A#1 16
A#1 16	A#1 16	A#1 16	A#1 4	- 2	- 8	G1 8	C2 16	F#1 16
G1 16	A#1 16	C2 16	F#1 16	G1 16	A#1 16	C2 16	A#1 16	G1 16
F1 16	D#1 16	C1 16	D#1 16	F1 16	G1 2	- 4	- 8	C2 4
A#1 16	C2 16	D2 16	C2 16	G1 16	C2 16	D2 16	C2 2	

BABA O'RILEY

Words & Music by Pete Townshend

© Copyright 1971 Fabulous Music Limited, Suite 2.07,
Plaza 535 King's Road, London SW10 0SZ.
All Rights Reserved. International Copyright Secured.

F#1 16	F#1 16	C#2 16	C#2 16	F#2 16		TEMPO 112
F#2 16	C#2 16	C#2 16	F#1 16	F#1 16	C#2 16	C#2 16	F#2 16	F#2 16
C#2 16	C#2 16	F#1 16	F#1 16	C#2 16	C#2 16	F#2 16	F#2 16	C#2 16
C#2 16	F#1 16	F#1 16	C#2 16	C#2 16	F#2 16	F#2 16	C#2 16	C#2 16
C#2 32	D#2 32	C#2 32	D#2 32	C#2 32	D#2 32	C#2 32	D#2 32	F#2 4
- 4	C#2 32	D#2 32	C#2 32	D#2 32	C#2 32	D#2 32	C#2 16	F#2 4

THE BAD TOUCH

Words & Music by Jimmy Pop

© Copyright 1999 The Jimmy Franks Publishing Company/Hey Rudy Music Publishing
Incorporated/Universal-Songs Of PolyGram International Incorporated, USA. Universal Music
Publishing Limited, Elsinore House, 77 Fulham Palace Road, London W6 8JA.
All Rights Reserved. International Copyright Secured.

C2 8	C2 8	C2 4	C2 8	C2 8		TEMPO 140
D2 4	D#2 8	D#2 8	D#2 8	F2 8	D#2 8	D#2 8	D#2 4	D2 8
D2 8	D2 8	D2 8	D2 8	D2 8	D2 8	D2 8	D#2 8	D#2 8
F2 8	D#2 8	D#2 4.	G2 8	G2 2	G2 8	G#2 8	G2 8	C2 8
A#1 4	- 4	G2 8	G#2 8	G2 8	A#2 8	A#1 4	- 4	G2 8
G#2 8	G2 8	D#2 8.	D#2 8.	D#2 8.	D#2 8	F2 16	D#2 16	F2 8

CENTREFOLD

Words & Music by Seth Justman

© Copyright 1981 Center City Music/Pal-Park Music, USA.
Warner/Chappell Music Limited, Griffin House, 161 Hammersmith Road, London W6 8BS
(75%)/Rondor Music (London) Limited, 10A Parsons Green, London SW6 4TW (25%).
All Rights Reserved. International Copyright Secured.

B1 4	D2 8.	B1 16	A1 8	G1 8			TEMPO 112
G1 8.	G1 16	E1 8	G1 8	G1 8	E1 16	G1 16	A1 8	G1 8
G1 8	A1 8	B1 4	D2 8.	B1 16	A1 8	G1 8	G1 8.	G1 16
E1 8	G1 8	G1 8	E1 16	G1 16	A1 8	G1 8	G1 4

CRAZY TRAIN

Words & Music by Ozzy Osbourne, Bob Daisley & Randy Rhoads

© Copyright 1980 Blizzard Music Limited, Regent House, 1 Pratt Mews, London NW1 0AD.
All Rights Reserved. International Copyright Secured.

F#1 8	F#1 8	C#2 8	C#2 8	D2 8			TEMPO 160
D2 8	B1 8	B1 8	B1 8	A1 8	G#1 8	A1 8	B1 8	A1 8
G#1 8	E1 8	F#1 8	F#1 8	C#2 8	C#2 8	D2 8	D2 8	B1 8
B1 8	B1 8	A1 8	G#1 8	A1 8	A1 8	A1 8	G#1 8	E1 8
F#1 8

THE HINDU TIMES

Words & Music by Noel Gallagher

© Copyright 2002 Oasis Music/Creation Songs Limited/Sony/ATV Music Publishing (UK) Limited, 10 Great Marlborough Street, London W1F 7LP.
All Rights Reserved. International Copyright Secured.

B1	D#2	E2	D#2	E2			TEMPO
4	8	8	32	32			112

D#2	B1	B1	D#2	E2	F#2	E2	D#2	B1
8	4	8	8	8	8	8	4	4

D#2	E2	D#2	E2	D#2	B1	A1	A1	A1
8	8	32	32	8	4	4	8

A1	B1	B1
8	8	4

BEATING AROUND THE BUSH

Words & Music by Bon Scott, Malcolm Young & Angus Young

© Copyright 1979 J. Albert & Son Pty. Limited for the world. Used by permission.
All Rights Reserved. International Copyright Secured.

E1	G1	A1	A#1	B1			TEMPO
16	16	16	16	16			112

D2	-	E1	G1	A1	A#1	B1	D2	-
2.	1	16	16	16	16	16	2.	1

E1	G1	A1	A#1	B1	D2	B1	A#1	A1
16	16	16	16	16	16	16	16	16

G1	E1	G1	E1	E1	E2	E1	G1	A1
16	16	16	16	16	8	16	16	16

A#1	B1	D2	B1	A#1	A1	G1	E1	E2
16	16	16	16	16	16	16	16	4.

PAPERCUT

Words & Music by Chester Bennington, Rob Bourdon, Brad Delson, Joseph Hahn & Mike Shinoda

© Copyright 2000 Zomba Songs Incorporated/Big Bad Mr. Hahn Music/Nondisclosure Agreement Music/Rob Bourdon Music/Kenji Kobayashi Music/Zomba Enterprises Incorporated/Chesterchaz Publishing, USA. Zomba Music Publishers Limited, 165-167 High Road, London NW10 2SG. All Rights Reserved. International Copyright Secured.

C#2 8	G#1 8	D#2 8	G#1 8	E2 8			TEMPO 180
G#1 8	D#2 8	G#1 8	C#2 8	G#1 8	D#2 8	G#1 8	E2 8	G#1 8
D#2 8	G#1 8	C#2 8	G#1 8	D#2 8	G#1 8	E2 8	G#1 8	D#2 8
G#1 8	C#2 8	G#1 8	D#2 8	G#1 8	E2 8	G#1 8	D#2 8	G#1 8
C#2 4							

PARANOID

Words & Music by Ozzy Osbourne, Tony Iommi, Terry 'Geezer' Butler & Bill Ward

© Copyright 1970 Westminster Music Limited, Suite 2.07, Plaza 535 King's Road, London SW10 0SZ. All Rights Reserved. International Copyright Secured.

E1 4	- 8	E1 4	- 8	E1 4			TEMPO 160
A1 8	B1 8	D2 8	E2 8	A1 8	B1 8	D2 8	E2 8	E1 4
- 8	E1 4	- 8	E1 4	A1 8	B1 8	D2 8	E2 8	A1 4
B1 8	D2 8	E2 8	G2 8	G2 4	G2 4	G2 4	G2 4	E2 4
E2 4	E2 4	D2 4	D2 4	D2 4	F#2 4	- 8	F#2 8	E2 4
E2 4							

PARTY HARD

Words & Music by Andrew W.K.

© Copyright 2001 Andrew WK Music/Songs Of Universal Incorporated, USA. Universal Music Publishing Limited, Elsinore House, 77 Fulham Palace Road, London W6 8JA. All Rights Reserved. International Copyright Secured.

G#1 4	E1 2	- 8	A1 4	E1 2			TEMPO 160
- 8	B1 4	E1 2	- 8	D#2 4	E2 4	E2 2	G#1 4	E1 2
- 8	A1 4	E1 2	- 8	B1 4	E1 2	- 8	F#2 4	G#2 4
E2 2	E2 8	E2 8	E2 8	E2 8	E2 8	- 8	B2 8	- 8
A2 8	A2 8	A2 8	- 8	G#2 8	G#2 8	G#2 8	- 8	F#2 8
F#2 8	F#2 8	F#2 8	F#2 4	C#3 4	B2 8	B2 8	B2 8	E2 2

THE SPIRIT OF RADIO

Words by Neil Peart

Music by Geddy Lee & Alex Lifeson

© Copyright 1980 Core Music Publishing Company, Canada. Carlin Music Corporation, Iron Bridge House, 3 Bridge Approach, London NW1 8BD. All Rights Reserved. International Copyright Secured.

F#1 16	E1 16	D1 16	E1 16	A1 16			TEMPO 100
E1 16	D1 16	E1 16	F#1 16	E1 16	D1 16	E1 16	G#1 16	E1 16
D1 16	E1 8.	F#1 16	- 16	G1 8	G#1 16	A1 8.	B1 16	- 16
C2 16	C#2 16	E2 16	E1 8.	F#1 16	- 16	G1 8	G#1 16	A1 8.
B1 16	- 16	C2 16	C#2 16	E2 16	E1 8.		

SUNBURN

Lyrics & Music by Matthew Bellamy

© Copyright 1999 Taste Music Limited, 1 Prince Of Wales Passage, 117 Hampstead Road, London NW1 3EF. All Rights Reserved. International Copyright Secured.

B1 16	B2 16	G2 16	E2 16	B2 16			TEMPO 100
G2 16	E2 16	G2 16	A1 16	B2 16	E2 16	C2 16	B2 16	E2 16
C2 16	E2 16	C2 16	C3 16	G2 16	E2 16	C3 16	G2 16	E2 16
G2 16	A1 16	B2 16	E2 16	C2 16	B2 16	E2 16	C2 16	E2 16

VEGAS TWO TIMES

Words & Music by Kelly Jones

© Copyright 2001 Stereophonics Music Limited/Universal Music Publishing Limited. Elsinore House, 77 Fulham Palace Road, London W6 8JA. All Rights Reserved. International Copyright Secured.

D2 4	C2 16	A1 16	A1 16	C2 16			TEMPO 90
A1 16	A1 16	C2 16	A1 16	C2 16	D2 16	D2 16	C2 16	F#1 8.
G1 8.	G#1 8.	A1 8.	C2 8	C#2 8	D2 4	C2 16	A1 16	A1 16
C2 16	A1 16	A1 16	C2 16	A1 16	C2 16	D2 16	D2 16	C2 16
F#1 8.	G1 8.	G#1 8.	A1 8.	C2 8	C#2 8	D2 4		

WATERFALL

Words & Music by John Squire & Ian Brown

© Copyright 1989 Zomba Music Publishers Limited, 165-167 High Road, London NW10 2SG. All Rights Reserved. International Copyright Secured.

F#1 8.	F#2 8	F#1 16	C#2 8	B1 8			TEMPO 112
B1 8	A#1 8	B1 8	F#1 8.	F#2 8	F#1 16	C#2 8	B1 8	B1 8
A#1 8	B1 8	F#1 8.	F#2 8	F#1 16	C#2 8	B1 8	B1 8	A#1 8
B1 8	F#1 8.	F#2 8	F#1 16	C#2 8	B1 8	B1 8	A#1 8	B1 8
F#1 8.

YOUTH OF THE NATION

Words & Music by Marcos Curiel, Mark Daniels,
Paul Sandoval & Noah Bernardo

© Copyright 2001 Souljah Music/Famous Music Corporation, USA. All Rights Reserved. International Copyright Secured.

G1 8	G1 8	F1 8	G1 8	D#1 2			TEMPO 100
- 4	D#1 16	F1 8	F1 16	D#1 16	G1 16	G#1 8	G1 8	- 16
G1 8	G1 8	F1 8	G1 8	D#1 2	- 4	D#1 16	F1 8	F1 16
D#1 16	F1 16	D#1 8	C1 4

CAN'T TAKE MY EYES OFF YOU

Words & Music by Bob Crewe & Bob Gaudio

© Copyright 1967 EMI Longitude Music Company/Seasons Four Music Corporation, USA.
EMI Music Publishing Limited, 127 Charing Cross Road, London WC2H OQY (50%)/
EMI Music Publishing (WP) Limited, 127 Charing Cross Road, London WC2H OQY
(50%) for the United Kingdom and the Republic of Ireland.
All Rights Reserved. International Copyright Secured.

G#1 4	A1 8	- 8	G#1 4	A1 8		**TEMPO 125**
- 8	G#1 4	A1 8	C2 8	- 8	B1 8	- 8	A1 8	G#1 4
A1 8	- 8	G#1 4	A1 8	- 8	C2 1	- 4	E2 4	E2 4
E2 4	E2 4	A1 8	B1 4.	C2 8	D2 8	E2 8	E2 4	D2 4
C2 8	B1 8	C2 8	D2 4	G1 4.	A1 8	B1 8	C2 8	D2 8
D2 4	C2 4	B1 8	A1 8	B1 4	C2 4	F1 2		

GREEN ONIONS

By Booker T. Jones, Steve Cropper, Al Jackson Jr. & Lewie Steinberg

© Copyright 1962 East Publications Incorporated, USA. All rights for the world (excluding USA)
assigned to Progressive Music Publishing Company Incorporated, USA. Carlin Music
Corporation, Iron Bridge House, 3 Bridge Approach, London NW1 8BD for the United
Kingdom, the Republic of Ireland, South Africa, Israel and the British Dominions, Colonies,
Overseas Territories & Dependencies. All Rights Reserved. International Copyright Secured.

C2 16	F1 4	F2 4	D#2 4	D2 8.			**TEMPO 140**
C2 16	F1 4	F2 4	D#2 4	D2 8.	C2 16	F1 4	F2 4	D#2 4
D2 8.	C2 16	F1 4	F2 4	D#2 4	D2 8.	F2 16	A#1 4	D2 4
C#2 4	D#2 8.	F2 16	A#1 4	D2 4	C#2 4	D#2 8.	F2 16	F1 4
F2 4	D#2 4	D2 8.	C2 16	F1 4	F2 4	D#2 4	D2 8.	C2 4
C2 4	D#2 4	F2 4	A#1 4	A#1 4	C#2 4	D#2 8.	F2 16	F1 4

SOUL BOSSA NOVA
By Quincy Jones

© Copyright 1963 Silhouette Music Corporation, USA.
Warner/Chappell Music Limited, Griffin House, 161 Hammersmith Road, London W6 8BS.
All Rights Reserved. International Copyright Secured.

C#2 8	- 4	C#2 8	C#2 8	- 4			TEMPO 140
C#2 8	C#2 8	- 8	C#2 4	- 8	F1 8	C#2 8	C#2 8	A#1 8
A#1 8	- 4	- 8	F1 8	C#2 8	C#2 8	A#1 8	A#1 8	- 4
- 8	F1 8	C#2 8	C#2 8	A#1 8	A#1 8	- 4	- 8	F1 8
C#2 8	C#2 8	A#1 8	A#1 8

I FEEL FINE
Words & Music by John Lennon & Paul McCartney

© Copyright 1964 Northern Songs.
All Rights Reserved. International Copyright Secured.

G1 4	G2 4	G2 8	F2 8	D2 8			TEMPO 180
C3 4	B2 4	A2 4	B2 8	- 8	C2 8	D2 4	F2 4	C2 4
B1 8	C2 4.	B1 8	C2 4.	C#2 8	D2 4.	F2 4	C2 4	B1 8
C2 4.	B1 8	C2 4.	C#2 8	D2 4.	D2 4	- 1	- 2	D2 4
D2 4	D2 4	D2 8	C2 4.	C2 8	A#1 4	C2 8	A#1 4	G1 1

I WANT YOU BACK

Words & Music by Frederick Perren, Alphonso Mizell,
Deke Richards & Berry Gordy Jr.

© Copyright 1969 Jobete Music Company Incorporated, USA. Jobete Music (UK) Limited,
127 Charing Cross Road, London WC2H 0GY for the United Kingdom & the
Republic of Ireland. All Rights Reserved. International Copyright Secured.

A1	-	-	-	-		TEMPO
8	8	4	8	16		100

C2	C#2	E2	F#2	D2	-	-	-	B1
16	16	16	16	8	8	4	16	16

C#2	D2	D#2	E2	F2	F#2	C#2	D2	-
16	8	16	16	16	4	4	16	16

-	A1	-	B1	E2	A1	-	E2	F#2
16	8.		4	8.	16		16	16

A2	F#2	A2
16	16	16

LILY THE PINK

Traditional

Arranged & Adapted by John Gorman, Roger McGough & Mike McGear

© Copyright 1968 Noel Gay Music Company Limited, 8/9 Frith Street, London W1D 3JB.
All Rights Reserved. International Copyright Secured.

G1.	E1	E1	E1	E1		TEMPO
8.	8	16	8	16		90

E1	G1	G1	F1	E1	D1	D1	D1	D1
8	16	16	16	16	8	16	8	16

D1	D1	D1	E1	F1	A1	A1	G1	F1
8	16	8	16	2	16	16	16	16

E1	C2	G1	-	G1	G1	F1	E1	E1
8	16	4	16	16	8	16	8.	4

-	G1	G1	F1	E1	D1	D1	-	D1
16	16	16	16	16	8.	4	16	16

D1	E1	F1	F1	-	F1	E1	D1	C1
8	16	8.	4	16	16	8	16	2

LIQUIDATOR

By Harry Johnson

© Copyright 1969 Cari Blue Music Limited, 10 Roosevelt Avenue,
Kingston 6, Jamaica, West Indies.
All Rights Reserved. International Copyright Secured.

D#1 **4**	E1 **4**	F#1 **4**	B1 **2**	F#2 **4**		TEMPO **180**
E2 **1**	D2 **8**	C#2 **8**	B1 **2.**	- **2**	D#1 **4**	E1 **4**	F#1 **2**	B1 **4**
F#2 **4**	E2 **1**	D2 **8**	C#2 **8**	B1 **2**	G#1 **4**	B1 **1**	- **1**	E2 **8**
C#2 **8**	B1 **8**	G#1 **8**	E2 **8**	C#2 **8**	B1 **8**	G#1 **8**	E2 **8**	C#2 **8**
B1 **8**	G#1 **8**	E2 **8**	C#2 **8**	B1 **8**	G#1 **8**	B1 **8**	- **8**	B1 **8**
- **8**	B1 **8**

LIVING IN THE PAST

Words & Music by Ian Anderson

© Copyright 1969 Ian Anderson Music Limited/Chrysalis Music Limited, The Chrysalis
Building, Bramley Road, London W10 6SP
All Rights Reserved. International Copyright Secured.

C2 **8**	G1 **4**	C1 **8**	D#1 **8**	G1 **8**		TEMPO **140**
F1 **4**	F2 **4**	C2 **8**	G1 **4**	C1 **8**	D#1 **8**	G1 **8**	F1 **4**	F2 **4**
G1 **2.**	F1 **4**	A#1 **4**	A1 **4**	G1 **8**	G1 **4.**	- **2**	G1 **2.**	F1 **4**
A#1 **4**	A1 **4**	G1 **8**	G1 **4.**	- **2**	C2 **2.**	A#1 **4**	A1 **4**	G1 **4**
F1 **8**	G1 **4.**	- **2**	C2 **2.**	A#1 **4**	A1 **4**	G1 **4**	F1 **8**	G1 **4.**

THE MIGHTY QUINN

Words & Music by Bob Dylan

© Copyright 1968, 1976 Dwarf Music, USA.
This arrangement © Copyright 2002 Dwarf Music.
All Rights Reserved. International Copyright Secured.

F#2 8	- 8	F#2 8	- 16	F#2 16			**TEMPO 100**
G#2 16	F#2 8.	D#2 8	C#2 8	B1 8	B1 4	B1 2	- 8	B1 16
B1 8.	- 8	G#1 16	B1 4	- 16	- 4	C#2 16	C#2 8.	- 8
B1 16	B1 4	- 16	- 8	F#2 8	F#2 16	- 16	- 8	F#2 16
- 8	F#2 16	G#2 16	F#2 8.	D#2 8	C#2 8	B1 8	B1 4	B1 8

NUT ROCKER

By Peter Ilyich Tchaikovsky
Arranged by Kim Fowley

© Copyright 1962 Kim Fowley Music. Ardmore & Beechwood Limited,
127 Charing Cross Road, London WC2H OQY.
All Rights Reserved. International Copyright Secured.

E2 8	D2 8	D2 8	E2 8	E2 8			**TEMPO 180**
- 8	E2 8	D2 8	D2 8	D2 8	E2 8	- 8	G1 8	G1 8
G1 8	C2 4.	D2 8	C2 4	B1 4	A1 4	G1 4	F#1 4	A1 4
B1 4.	C2 8	B1 4	A1 4	G1 4	F#1 4	E1 4	B1 4	A1 4
G1 4	F#1 4	A1 4	G1 4	F#1 4	E1 4	B1 4	C2 4	B1 4
A1 4	G1 4	F#1 4	E1 4	D1 4				

RETURN OF DJANGO

By Lee 'Scratch' Perry

© Copyright 1969 New Town Sound Limited.
B & C Music Publishing Limited, Regent House, 1 Pratt Mews, London NW1 0AD.
All Rights Reserved. International Copyright Secured.

C#2 4	A#1 16	G#1 16	E1 4	C#1 8			TEMPO 200
- 4	- 8	C#2 4	A#1 16	G#1 16	E1 4	C#1 8	- 1	- 8
C#2 4	A#1 16	G#1 16	E1 4	C#1 8	- 4	- 8	C#2 4	A#1 16
G#1 16	E1 4	C#1 8	- 2	- 4	C2 8	C2 8	C2 8	C2 8
C2 8	C2 8	C2 8	C2 8	C2 8	C2 8	C2 8	C2 8	D#2 8

SPANISH FLEA

By Julius Wechter

© Copyright 1965 Almo Music Corporation, USA.
Rondor Music (London) Limited, 10A Parsons Green, London SW6 4TW (75%)/
Burlington Music Company Limited, Griffin House, 161 Hammersmith Road, London
W6 8BS (25%). All Rights Reserved. International Copyright Secured.

D2 8	D#1 8	E1 8	F1 8	- 8			TEMPO 160
D2 8	A#1 8	D2 8	C2 4	B1 2	- 4	G1 8	F#1 8	F1 8
E1 8	- 8	C2 8	A#1 8	C2 8	A#1 4	A1 2	- 4	F1 8
E1 8	D#1 8	D1 8	F1 8	A#1 8	G1 4	A#1 8	C2 8	- 8
F1 8	G#1 8	C#2 4	A#1 8	C#2 8	D#2 8	- 8	F2 1	- 4
F2 8	F2 8	G2 8	F2 8	C#2 16	C2 8.	A#1 8		

SUSPICIOUS MINDS

Words & Music by Francis Zambon

© Copyright 1969 Sony/ATV Songs LLC, USA. Sony/ATV Music Publishing (UK) Limited, 10 Great Marlborough Street, London W1F 7LP. All Rights Reserved. International Copyright Secured.

D1 8	B1 8	B1 8	G1 8	D1 16			TEMPO 112
E1 16	C2 16	E1 16	C2 16	E1 8	D1 8	B1 8	B1 8	D1 8
D1 16	E1 16	C2 16	E1 16	C2 8	D1 8	C1 8	E1 8	E1 8
C1 8	G1 16	A1 16	F2 16	A1 16	F2 8	A1 8	G1 8	E2 8
E2 8	C2 8	G1 16	A1 16	F2 16	A1 16	F2 8	A1 8	

A SWINGIN' SAFARI

Words & Music by Burt Kaempfert & June Tansey

© Copyright 1962 Screen Gems-EMI Music Incorporated, USA. Screen Gems-EMI Music Limited, 127 Charing Cross Road, London WC2H 0QY. All Rights Reserved. International Copyright Secured.

A#1 16	D#2 8.	G2 16	- 16	A#1 16			TEMPO 112
D#2 8.	G2 16	- 16	C2 16	D#2 8.	G#2 16	- 16	C2 16	D#2 8.
G#2 16	- 16	A#1 16	D#2 8.	G2 16	- 16	A#1 16	D#2 8.	G2 16
- 16	A#1 16	D2 8	F2 16	D2 8	A#1 4	- 8	A#1 16	D#2 8.
G2 16	- 16	C2 16	D#2 8.	G#2 16	- 16	A#1 16	D#2 8.	G2 8
D#2 16	G#2 8	F2 16	D2 8	D#2 2			

(THERE'S) ALWAYS SOMETHING THERE TO REMIND ME

Words by Hal David Music by Burt Bacharach

© Copyright 1964 New Hidden Valley Music Company/Casa David, USA. Universal/ MCA Music Limited (50%)/Windswept Music (London) Limited (50%). All Rights Reserved. International Copyright Secured.

D#1	C2	C#2	-	A#1			TEMPO
8	8	8	8	2			160

D#1	C2	C#2	-	D#2	D#1	C2	A#1	-
8	8	8	2	8	8	8	8	8

G#1	-	C2	C2	C#2	C2	A#1	C2	C#2
1	1	4	4	4	4	4	4	8

C2	A#1	-	-	G#1	F1	-	D#1	C1
4	4	4	8	4.	8	8	4.	4.

-	C2	C2	C#2	C2	A#1	C2	C#2	C2
4	4	4	4	8	4	4	4	4

A#1	-	-	G#1	F1	-	D#1	C1
4	4	8	4.	8	8	4.	4.

WIPE OUT

By Ron Wilson, James Fuller, Bob Berryhill & Pat Connolly

© Copyright 1963 Miraleste Music/Robin Hood Music Company, USA. Ambassador Music Limited, 22 Denmark Street, London WC2H 8NG. All Rights Reserved. International Copyright Secured.

F1	A#1	B1	C2	C2			TEMPO
8	8	8	8	8			180

C2	A#1	G1	G1	C2	B1	A#1	A#1	A#1
8	8	8	8	8	8	8	8	8

G#1	F1	C1	D#1	E1	F1	F1	F1	D#1
8	8	8	8	8	8	8	8	8

C1	C1	D#1	E1	F1	C2	-	C2	-
8	8	8	8	8	8	8	8	8

C2	-	C2	F2
8	8	8	8

ALL THE WAY FROM MEMPHIS

Words & Music by Ian Hunter

© Copyright 1973 Island Music Limited. Universal/Island Music Limited,
Elsinore House, 77 Fulham Palace Road, London W6 8JA.
All Rights Reserved. International Copyright Secured.

F#1 8	F#1 8	F1 4	D#1 4	F1 8				TEMPO 125
D#1 8	- 8	C#1 8	- 8	C#1 4	C#1 8	C#1 8	C#1 8	F#1 8
F#1 8	F1 8	- 8	D#1 8	F1 8	D#1 8	- 8	C#1 4.	- 4
- 4	F#2 8	F#2 8	F2 8	- 8	D#2 4	F2 8	D#2 8	- 8
C#2 8	- 8	C#2 4	C#2 8	C#2 8	C#2 8	F#2 8	F#2 8	F2 8
- 8	D#2 4	F2 8	D#2 8	- 8	C#2 8	- 8	C#2 4.	

ARRIVAL

By Benny Andersson & Björn Ulvaeus

© Copyright 1976 Union Songs AB, Stockholm, Sweden for the world. Bocu Music Limited,
1 Wyndham Yard, Wyndham Place, London W1H 1AR for Great Britain and the
Republic of Ireland. All Rights Reserved. International Copyright Secured.

F2 2	F2 2	F2 8	F#2 8	F2 16				TEMPO 112
D#2 16	C#2 8	D#2 4	C#2 8	C2 8	A#1 4	G#1 4	A#1 4	C2 4
C#2 1	- 4	F2 8	G#2 2	C#3 2	C#3 8	C#3 8	D#3 8	C#3 8
A#2 8	C3 2	A#2 2	A#2 8	C3 8	A#2 8	G#2 8	F2 2	- 4
C#2 8	D#2 8	F2 2	F2 2	F2 8	F#2 8	F2 16	D#2 16	C#2 8
D#2 4	C#2 8	C2 8	A#1 4	G#1 4	A#1 4	C2 4	C#2 2	

BLAME IT ON THE BOOGIE

Words & Music by Elmar Krohn, Thomas Meyer, Hans Kampschroer,
Michael Jackson Clark & David Jackson Rich

© Copyright 1977 Edition Delay/Fanfare Musikverlag, Germany. Global Chrysalis Music
Publishing Company Limited, The Chrysalis Building, 13 Bramley Road, London W10 6SP.
All Rights Reserved. International Copyright Secured.

D#2 16	- 16	**D#2** 16	- 16	**G1** 16			TEMPO **112**
- 16	**G1** 16	- 16	**C2** 16	- 16	**C2** 16	- 16	**G1** 16	- 16
G1 16	- 16	**F1** 16	- 16	**F1** 16	- 4	**G1** 16	- 16	**G#1** 16
- 16	**A1** 16	- 16	**A#1** 16	**C2** 16	**A#1** 16	**D#2** 16	- 16	**D#2** 16
- 16	**G1** 16	- 16	**G1** 16	- 16	**C2** 16	- 16	**C2** 16
G1 16	- 16	**G1** 16	- 16	**F1** 16	- 16	**F1** 16	

CAROLINE

Words & Music by Francis Rossi & Robert Young

© Copyright 1973 Valley Music Limited, Elsinore House,
77 Fulham Palace Road, London W6 8JA.
All Rights Reserved. International Copyright Secured.

C1 8	**C1** 8	**D1** 8	**C1** 8	**D#1** 8			TEMPO **180**
C1 8	**D1** 8	**C1** 8	**C1** 8	**C1** 8	**D1** 8	**C1** 8	**D#1** 8	**C1** 8
D1 8	**C1** 8	**F1** 8	**F1** 8	**A#1** 8	**F1** 8	**A1** 8	**F1** 8	**A#1** 8
A1 4	**F1** 8	**A#1** 8	**F1** 8	**A1** 8	**F1** 8	**A#1** 8	**G#1** 4	**F1** 8
A#1 8	**F1** 8	**G#1** 8	**F1** 8	**A#1** 8	**G#1** 4	**F1** 8	**A#1** 8	**F1** 8
G#1 8	**F1** 8	**A#1** 8	**A1** 4	**F1** 8	**A#1** 8	**F1** 8	**A1** 4

CROCODILE ROCK

Words & Music by Elton John & Bernie Taupin

© Copyright 1972 Dick James Music Limited. Universal/Dick James Music Limited, Elsinore House, 77 Fulham Palace Road, London W6 8JA. All Rights Reserved. International Copyright Secured.

B1 8	B1 8	B1 8	B1 8	B1 8			**TEMPO 140**
B1 4	G1 8	B1 8	G1 8	C2 8	B1 4.	- 4	B1 8	B1 8
B1 8	B1 8	B1 8	B1 8	G1 8	B1 8	G1 8	C2 8	B1 4.
- 4	C2 8	C2 8	C2 8	C2 8	C2 8	C2 4	G1 8	C2 8
G1 8	D2 8	C2 4.	- 4	D2 8	D2 8	D2 8	D2 8	D2 8
D2 4	B1 8	D2 8	B1 8	E2 8	D2 4.

DOUBLE BARREL

Words & Music by Winston Riley

© Copyright 1971 Prophesy Music Publishing Company, administered worldwide by Westbury Music Limited, Suite B, 2 Tunstall Road, London SW9 8DA. All Rights Reserved. International Copyright Secured.

A#2 4	- 8	D3 8	- 8.	F3 8			**TEMPO 140**
- 16	- 32	F#3 32	G3 4.	D#3 8	- 8	F3 4	- 4	- 1
- 1	A#1 4	- 8	D2 8	- 8	F2 8	- 8	D2 32	D#2 4.
C2 8	- 8	D2 8	D2 8	D2 8

EGYPTIAN REGGAE

By Jonathan Richman & Earl Johnson

© Copyright 1977 Modern Love Songs/Snapping Turtle Music/Soul Syndicate Music, USA.
Hornall Brothers Music Limited, The Basement, 754 Fulham Road, London SW6 5SH
(50%)/Bug Music Limited, 31 Milson Road, London W14 0LJ (50%).
All Rights Reserved. International Copyright Secured.

A1 8	C2 8	D2 8	- 8	D2 8			TEMPO 100
C2 8	A1 8	- 8	A1 8	C2 8	D2 8	F2 8	D2 8	C2 8
A1 8	- 8	A1 8	C2 8	D2 8	- 8	D2 8	C2 8	A1 8
- 8	A1 8	C2 8	D2 8	F2 8	D2 8	C2 8	A1 8	- 8
A1 8	C2 8	G1 8	- 8	A#1 8	C2 8	A1 8	- 8	C2 8
D2 8	G1 8	- 8	A#1 8	C2 8	A1 8	- 8	C2 4	D2 8

FLASHLIGHT

Words & Music by George Clinton, Bernard Worrell & William Collins

© Copyright 1978 Bridgeport Music Incorporated (66.67%)/Rubber Band Music
Incorporated, USA. Universal/Island Music Limited, Elsinore House, 77 Fulham Palace
Road, London W6 8JA (33.33%).
All Rights Reserved. International Copyright Secured.

C2 8.	- 16	D2 8.	- 16	D#2 8.			TEMPO 100
F2 16	- 16	F2 16	- 8	G2 8.	- 16	G2 8.	D#2 16	G2 16
D#2 16	- 16	G2 16	- 16	A2 16	- 8	G2 8.	- 16	G2 8
- 16	D#2 16	G2 16	A2 16	- 8	- 16	G1 32	A#1 16.	G1 32
C2 16	- 16	C2 16	- 16	A#1 16	- 16	A#1 16	- 16	G1 16
- 16	G1 16	- 16	F#1 16	- 16	F#1 16	- 16	F1 16	

THAT'S THE WAY (I LIKE IT)

Words & Music by Harry Casey & Richard Finch

© Copyright 1975 Longitude Music Company, USA. EMI Music Publishing (WP) Limited, 127 Charing Cross Road, London WC2H OQY for the United Kingdom and the Republic of Ireland. All Rights Reserved. International Copyright Secured.

C2 4.	D2 4.	D#2 4.	G2 4.	- 32			TEMPO 225
D#2 4	D2 4	C2 4.	A#1 4.	C2 2.	- 4	- 8	C2 4.	D2 4.
D#2 4.	G2 4.	- 32	D#2 4	D2 4	C2 4.	A#1 4.	C2 2	C1 16
D1 16	D#1 16	E1 16	F1 16	F#1 16	G1 16	A1 16	A#1 16	B1 16
C2 16	C#2 16	D2 16	D#2 4.	C2 8	C2 4	A#1 4	C2 4	A#1 4
C2 4	C2 4	F2 4.	D#2 4	- 8	A#1 4	C2 4	A#1 4	C2 4

IF I CAN'T HAVE YOU

Words & Music by Barry Gibb, Maurice Gibb & Robin Gibb

© Copyright 1978 Gibb Brothers Music. All Rights Reserved. International Copyright Secured.

E1 8.	F1 8.	G1 8	G1 4.	F1 16			TEMPO 112
E1 16	F1 2	E1 8.	F1 8.	G1 8	A1 8.	G1 8.	F1 8	E1 4
C1 8	C1 4.	G1 8	F1 2	F2 16	E2 16	D2 16	A1 4.	G1 4.
- 4	C2 16	A#1 16	A1 4.	A#1 4.	F1 4.	F2 8	F2 8	F2 8
F2 8

PICK UP THE PIECES

**By Roger Ball, Hamish Stuart, Alan Gorrie, Onnie McIntyre,
Malcolm Duncan & Robert McIntosh**

© Copyright 1974 Average Music/Bug Music Limited, 31 Milson Road, London W14 OLJ
(75%)/Joe's Songs/Fairwood Music Limited, 72 Marylebone Lane, London W1U 2PL (25%).
All Rights Reserved. International Copyright Secured.

G#1 16	C2 16	G2 16	F2 16	- 8			TEMPO 112
D#2 16	A#1 16	D2 16	C2 16	- 8	A#2 16	G#2 16	F2 16	G#2 8.
F2 16	- 16	D#2 16	F2 16	- 16	G#2 8.	F2 16	- 16	D#2 16
F2 16	- 8	F2 16	- 16	G2 16	G#2 16	- 8	A#2 16	G#2 8.
F2 16	- 8	C2 16	D#2 16	E2 16	F2 16	- 16	G2 16	G#2 16
- 8	A#2 16	G#2 8.

POPCORN

By Gershon Kingsley

© Copyright 1969 & 1971 Bourne Company, USA.
Bourne Music Limited, 2nd Floor, 207-209 Regent Street, London W1B 4ND.
All Rights Reserved. International Copyright Secured.

B2 16	- 16	A2 16	- 16	B2 16			TEMPO 125
- 16	F#2 16	- 16	D2 16	- 16	F#2 16	- 16	B1 16	- 16
- 8	B2 16	- 16	A2 16	- 16	B2 16	- 16	F#2 16	- 16
D2 16	- 16	F#2 16	- 16	B1 16	- 16	- 8	B2 8	C#3 8
D3 8	C#3 8	D3 8	B2 8	C#3 8	B2 8	C#3 8	A2 8	B2 8
A2 8	B2 8	G2 8	B2 8

S.O.S.

Words & Music by Benny Andersson, Björn Ulvaeus & Stig Anderson

© Copyright 1975 Union Songs AB, Stockholm, Sweden for the world.
Bocu Music Limited, 1 Wyndham Yard, Wyndham Place, London W1H 1AR for Great Britain
and the Republic of Ireland. All Rights Reserved. International Copyright Secured.

F2 8	A1 8	D2 8	F2 8	G2 8				TEMPO 225
C2 8	E2 8	G2 8	A2 8	C2 8	F2 8	A2 8	A#2 8	D2 8
G2 8	A#2 8	A2 8	C2 8	F2 8	A2 8	G2 8	C#2 8	E2 8
G2 8	F2 8	A1 8	D2 8	F2 8	E2 8	A1 8	C#2 8	E2 8
D2 2								

THIS TOWN AIN'T BIG ENOUGH FOR BOTH OF US

Words & Music by Ronald Mael

© Copyright 1974 Avenue Louise Music/EMI Virgin Music Limited,
127 Charing Cross Road, London WC2H 0QY.
All Rights Reserved. International Copyright Secured.

F1 16	- 16	F1 8	F1 16	- 16				TEMPO 125
F1 16	- 16	F1 8	F1 8	F1 16	F1 16	F1 8	E1 8	E1 4
- 2	A1 8	C2 8	E2 8	A2 8	C3 2	A#2 8	G2 4	D2 8
A#1 4	- 4	E1 8	F1 8	A#1 8	A1 8	- 8	- 4	- 8
F2 16	- 16	F2 8	F2 16	- 16	F2 8	F2 8	F2 8	F2 16
F2 16	F2 8	E2 8	E2 4					

WHISKEY IN THE JAR

Traditional

Arranged by Eric Bell, Brian Downey & Phil Lynott
© Copyright 1972 Pippin The Friendly Ranger Music Company Limited/Universal Music
Publishing Limited, Elsinore House, 77 Fulham Palace Road, London W6 8JA.
All Rights Reserved. International Copyright Secured.

| D2 | D2 | E2 | F#2 | G2 | | | TEMPO |
| 8 | 8 | 16 | 16 | 8 | | | 140 |

| E2 | F#2 | D2 | E2 | G2 | - | D2 | D2 | E2 |
| 8 | 8 | 8 | 8 | 2. | 4 | 8 | 8 | 16 |

| F#2 | G2 | E2 | F#2 | D2 | E2 | G2 | - | D2 |
| 16 | 8 | 8 | 8 | 8 | 8 | 2. | 4 | 8 |

| D2 | E2 | F#2 | G2 | E2 | F#2 | D2 | E2 | G2 |
| 8 | 16 | 16 | 8 | 8 | 8 | 8 | 8 | 2. |

| - | G1 | G1 | A1 | B1 | D2 | G1 | A1 | G1 |
| 4 | 8 | 8 | 16 | 16 | 8 | 8 | 8 | 8 |

| B1 | G1 |
| 8 | 2. |

YMCA

Words & Music by Jacques Morali, Henri Belolo & Victor Willis

© Copyright 1978 Scorpio Music, France.
EMI Music Publishing Limited, 127 Charing Cross Road, London WC2H 0QY.
All Rights Reserved. International Copyright Secured.

| A#1 | G#1 | D#1 | - | A#1 | | | TEMPO |
| 4. | 8 | 2 | 8 | 8 | | | 112 |

| G#1 | C#2 | A#1 | - | A#1 | G#1 | D#1 | - | A#2 |
| 8 | 16 | 16 | 16 | 16 | 8 | 8. | 16 | 4. |

| G#2 | D#2 | - | A#2 | G#2 |
| 8 | 2 | 8 | 8 | 8 |

| C#3 | A#2 | - | A#2 | G#2 |
| 16 | 16 | 16 | 16 | 8 |

| D#2 | - | F#2 | F#2 | F#2 |
| 8. | 16 | 4. | 16 | 16 |

| F#2 | F#2 | F#2 | F#2 |
| 4. | 16 | 16 | 2. |

BOYS DON'T CRY

Words by Robert Smith

Music by Robert Smith, Laurence Tolhurst & Michael Dempsey © Copyright 1979 Fiction
Songs Limited, Bedford House, 69-79 Fulham High Street, London SW6 3JW.
All Rights Reserved. International Copyright Secured.

C#2 4.	C#2 4	D2 8	E2 4	C#2 4.			TEMPO 160
C#2 4	D2 8	E2 4	E2 4.	E2 4	F#2 8	G#2 4	A2 4.	- 8
F#2 8	- 16	E2 8	- 16	D2 8	- 32	C#2 4.	C#2 4	D2 8
E2 4	C#2 4.	C#2 4	D2 8	E2 4	E2 4.	E2 4	F#2 8	G#2 4
A2 4.	- 8	F#2 8	- 16	E2 8	- 16	D2 8	- 32	C#2 2

THE CHAMP

By Harry Palmer

© Copyright 1968 The Sparta Florida Music Group Limited,
8/9 Frith Street, London W1D 3JB.
All Rights Reserved. International Copyright Secured.

C2 8	D#2 8	F2 8	- 8	C2 8			TEMPO 112
D#2 8	F2 8	- 8	C2 8	D#2 16	D2 16	C2 16	- 16	C2 8
- 2	C2 8	D#2 8	F2 8	- 8	C2 8	D#2 8	F2 8	- 8
C2 8	D#2 16	D2 16	C2 16	- 16	C2 8	- 4	F2 16	F2 16
G#2 16	A2 16	F2 16	C3 8	F2 16	A#2 16	F2 16	G#2 16	A2 16
F2 8	- 8	C2 8	E2 8	C2 16	G2 16	C2 8	F2 8	E2 8

COME BACK

Words & Music by Pete Wylie

© Copyright 1984 Universal Music Publishing Limited, Elsinore House,
77 Fulham Palace Road, London W6 8JA.
All Rights Reserved. International Copyright Secured.

F2 4	E2 2.	E2 4	E2 8	F2 4			TEMPO 140
F2 8	F2 4	E2 2.	F2 4	E2 8	E2 4	F2 8	F2 4
E2 4	F2 2.	E2 4	E2 8	F2 8	F2 4	F2 4	A2 4	G2 2
B2 2	C3 2	D3 2

COME INTO MY LIFE

Words & Music by Joyce Sims

© Copyright 1987 Hit And Hold Music Incorporated/Tawanne-Lamount Publishing, USA.
Chelsea Music Publishing Company Limited, 124 Great Portland Street, London W1N 5PG.
All Rights Reserved. International Copyright Secured.

B2 8	A#2 8	G#2 8	F#2 8	G#2 8			TEMPO 200
D#2 8	F#2 8	G#2 8	B2 8	A#2 8	G#2 8	F#2 8	G#2 8	D#2 8
F#2 8	G#2 8	D#2 8	D2 8	C#2 8
B1 8	C#2 8	B1 8	C#2 8	D#2 8
B1 2	G#1 2

(FEELS LIKE) HEAVEN

Words & Music by Kevin Patterson & Edward Jordan

© Copyright 1983 Carlin Music Corporation, Iron Bridge House, 3 Bridge Approach, London NW1 8BD. All Rights Reserved. International Copyright Secured.

D#1 8	F1 4	A#1 8	G1 4.	- 8			**TEMPO 112**
D#1 8	F1 4	A#1 8	G1 4.	D#1 4	G1 4.	C1 8	C1 2	- 2
- 4	- 8	D#1 8	F1 4	A#1 8	G1 4.	- 8	D#1 8	F1 4
A#1 8	G1 4.	A#1 4	C2 4.	D#2 8	D2 8	C2 4.	C2 2.

I CAN'T WAIT

Words & Music by John Smith

© Copyright 1986 Poolside Music Incorporated, USA. All Rights Reserved. International Copyright Secured.

C2 8	C2 8	D2 8	D#2 8	F2 8			**TEMPO 140**
- 8	F1 16	F1 16	F1 8	F1 8	F#1 8.	F#1 16	G1 8	- 8
G1 8	G1 4	- 8	A1 8	A#1 8	C2 16	G1 8	- 8	F1 8
F1 8	F1 16	- 16	F#1 16	G1 8	- 8	G1 8	G1 4	- 8
A1 8	#A1 8	C2 16	G1 8	- 8	F1 8	F1 8	F1 16	- 16
F#1 16	G1 8

IT MUST BE LOVE
Words & Music by Labi Siffre

© Copyright 1971 MAM (Music Publishing) Limited/Groovy Music Limited.
Chrysalis Songs Limited, The Chrysalis Building, Bramley Road, London W10 6SP.
All Rights Reserved. International Copyright Secured.

B1 4	A1 8	B1 4	A1 4.	G1 4.			TEMPO 220
E1 4.	G1 8	- 2	- 4	- 8	B1 8.	D2 4.	A1 8	- 4
- 8	D1 8	E1 8	B1 8	G1 4.	- 8	G1 4	- 8	D1 8
E1 4	D1 8	G1 4.	- 8	G1 4	- 8	D1 8	E1 4	D1 8
G1 4.	- 8	G1 4	- 8	D1 8	E1 4	D1 8	G1 4	G1 4
G1 4	G1 8	G1 8	G1 4	G#1 4			

JACK YOUR BODY
Words & Music by Steve 'Silk' Hurley

© Copyright 1986 Last Song Incorporated/Silktone Songs Incorporated, USA. The
International Music Network Limited, Independent House, 54 Larkshall Road, London E4 6PD
(75%)/Campbell Connelly & Company Limited, 8/9 Frith Street, London W1D 3JB (25%).
All Rights Reserved. International Copyright Secured.

G#1 4	G#1 8.	D#2 8	D#2 16	D#2 8			TEMPO 125
F#2 8	G#2 8	G#1 4	G#1 8.	D#2 8	D#2 16	D#2 8	F#2 8	D#2 8
G#1 4	G#1 8.	D#2 8	D#2 16	D#2 8	F#2 8	G#2 8	G#1 4	G#1 8.
D#2 8	G#1 16	C#2 16	G#1 16	B1 16	G#1 16	C#2 16	G#1 16	D#1 4
D#1 8.	A#1 8	D#1 16	G#1 16	D#1 16	F#1 16	D#1 16	G#1 16	C#1 16
D#1 4	D#1 8	A#1 16	D#1 16	G#1 16	D#1 16	F#1 16	C#1 8.	D#1 8

LET'S GROOVE

Words & Music by Maurice White & Wayne Vaughn

© Copyright 1981 Out Time Music/Saggifire Music, USA. Campbell Connelly & Company Limited, 8/9 Frith Street, London W1D 3JB (58.34%)/EMI Music Publishing Limited, 127 Charing Cross Road, London WC2H OQY (41.66%). All Rights Reserved. International Copyright Secured.

E1 4	- 8	G1 8	A1 4	G1 4			TEMPO 125
F#1 4	- 8	B1 4	A1 8	B1 4	E1 4	- 8	G1 8	A1 4
G1 4	F#1 4	- 8	B1 4	A1 8	B1 4	E1 8	- 8	D2 8
D2 8	B1 4	- 4	F#1 8	A1 8	C#2 8	B1 4	A1 8	D2 4
B1 8	- 8	D2 4	B1 4	- 4	C#2 8	A1 8	F#1 16.	A1 32
B1 4.

LIVING ON THE CEILING

Words & Music by Neil Arthur & Stephen Luscombe

© Copyright 1982 Cherry Red Music Limited. Complete Music Limited, 3rd Floor, Bishops Park House, 25-29 Fulham High Street, London SW6 3JH. All Rights Reserved. International Copyright Secured.

B1 8.	C2 8.	D2 8	C2 8.	B1 8.			TEMPO 112
D#2 8	E2 8.	F#2 8.	E2 8	D#2 4	- 4	B1 8.	C2 8.	D2 8
C2 8.	B1 8.	A1 8	B1 2.	- 4	B1 8.	C2 8.	D2 8	C2 8.
B1 8.	D#2 8	E2 8.	F#2 8.	E2 8	D#2 4	- 4	B1 8.	C2 8.
D2 8.	C2 8.	B1 8.	A1 8	B1 2.

MAKING YOUR MIND UP

Words & Music by Andy Hill & John Danter

© Copyright 1981 BMG Music Publishing Limited, Bedford House, 69-79 Fulham High Street, London SW6 3JW (50%)/RAK Publishing Limited, 42-48 Charlbert Street, London NW8 7BU (50%). All Rights Reserved. International Copyright Secured.

D2 4	B1 8	D2 4.	D2 4.	G1 4			TEMPO 180
- 4	- 8	B1 8	C2 4	C2 8	B1 8	D2 4.	D2 4.	G2 4
- 4	- 8	D2 8	D2 8	D2 8	E2 4.	E2 4	C2 4	C2 4
E2 4	E2 8	G2 4	F#2 8	E2 8	D2 8	- 4	D2 4	G1 4
G2 4	- 4	- 8	D2 8	D2 4	D2 8	F#2 4.	F#2 4	E2 4.
D2 8	- 4	- 8	G1 8	G1 8	G1 8	G1 8	G1 4.	G2 8

NELSON MANDELA

Words & Music by Jerry Dammers

© Copyright 1984 Plangent Visions Music Limited, 27 Noel Street, London W1F 8GZ. All Rights Reserved. International Copyright Secured.

C2 1	B1 2	- 8	A1 4	A1 4			TEMPO 140
G1 4	C2 4	G1 2	- 1	- 4	C2 1	B1 2	- 8	A1 4
A1 4	G1 4	C2 4	G1 2					

NEVER GONNA GIVE YOU UP

Words & Music by Mike Stock, Matt Aitken & Pete Waterman

© Copyright 1987 Sids Songs Limited/Universal Music Publishing Limited (33.34%)/
All Boys Music Limited (33.33%)/Mike Stock Publishing Limited (33.33%).
All Rights Reserved. International Copyright Secured.

G#1 16	A#1 16	C2 16	A#1 16	F2 8.		TEMPO 112
F2 8.	D#2 8	- 8	- 16	G#1 16	A#1 16	C2 16	A#1 16	D#2 8.
D#2 8.	C#2 8.	C2 16	A#1 16	- 16	G#1 16	A#1 16	C2 16	A#1 16
C#2 4	D#2 8	C2 8	A#1 8	G#1 8	- 8	G#1 8	D#2 4	C#2 4

HANDS UP (GIVE ME YOUR HEART)

Words & Music by Jean Kluger, Daniel Vangarde & Nelly Byl

© Copyright 1980 Zagora Editions Productions, France. R & E Music Limited/The International
Music Network Limited, Independent House, 54 Larkshall Road, London E4 6PD.
All Rights Reserved. International Copyright Secured.

B2 4	B2 4.	B2 4	A2 8	B2 4				TEMPO 180
B2 4.	A2 4	F#2 8	A2 4	B2 4	A2 8	F#2 8	E2 8	D2 8
4E 4	F#2 4	E2 8	D2 8	B1 8	A1 8	B2 4	B2 4.	B2 4
A2 8	B2 4	B2 4.	A2 4	F#2 8	A2 4	B2 4	A2 8	F#2 8
E2 8	D2 8	4E 4	F#2 4	E2 8	D2 8	B1 8	A1 8	B1 8
D2 8	D2 4	D2 8	G2 8	G2 4	G2 8	A2 8	E2 8	F#2 2

PARTY FEARS TWO

Words & Music by Billy MacKenzie & Alan Rankine

© Copyright 1982 Fiction Songs Limited, Bedford House,
69-79 Fulham High Street, London SW6 3JW.
All Rights Reserved. International Copyright Secured.

G2 4.	F#2 16	G2 16	F#2 8	D2 8			TEMPO 125
B1 8	A1 4	B1 8	C2 8	A1 4	G1 8	F1 8	E1 4	G1 8
C2 8	G1 8	D2 8	E2 8	- 8	A1 4	B1 8	C2 8	A1 8
D2 8	E2 8	D2 8	C2 8	D2 4.	D2 16	E2 16	F#2 4.	F#2 16
G2 16	A2 4.	A2 16	B2 16	C3 4	A2 4		

MOONLIGHT SHADOW

Words & Music by Mike Oldfield

© Copyright 1983 Oldfield Music Limited.
EMI Virgin Music Limited, 127 Charing Cross Road, London WC2H 0QY.
All Rights Reserved. International Copyright Secured.

C#2 8	D#2 8	E2 4.	E2 8	E2 8			TEMPO 140
E2 32	F#2 8	E2 8	D#2 8	C#2 2	C#2 2	D#2 8	D#2 8	E2 8
F#2 4.	E2 8	F#2 8	G#2 8	G#2 8	F#2 8	B1 8	- 8	G#2 4
G#2 8	A#2 32	B2 8	A2 8	G#2 8	G#2 4	F#2 8	F#2 8	G#2 8
F#2 2	G#2 4.	F#2 8	E2 4	E2 8	C#2 8	F#2 8	F#2 32	G#2 4
F#2 2							

THE BOX

By Paul Hartnoll & Phil Hartnoll

© Copyright 1996 Sony/ATV Music Publishing (UK) Limited,
10 Great Marlborough Street, London W1F 7LP.
All Rights Reserved. International Copyright Secured.

A1 8	A1 8	A1 8	A1 8	E2 4			TEMPO 140	
- 4	C2 4	- 8	B1 16	C2 16	A1 4	- 4	C2 8	C2 8
C2 8	C2 8	G2 4	- 4	C2 4	- 8	B1 16	C2 16	A1 4
B1 4	C2 2	- 4	- 8	B1 16	C2 16	A1 2	- 2	C2 2
- 4	- 8	C2 16	B1 16	A1 2				

CHILDREN

Words & Music by Roberto Concina

© Copyright 1996 Jeity Music, Italy.
All Rights Reserved. International Copyright Secured.

F2 1.	G#2 4	G2 8	D#2 1.	G#2 4			TEMPO 180	
G2 8	C2 1.	G#2 4	G2 8	G#1 1.	F1 16	G1 16	G#1 16	C2 16
F2 1.	G#2 4	G2 8	D#2 1.	C#2 16	C2 16	C#2 4	C2 8	G#1 2
G#1 8	G1 4	G#1 4	C2 8	F1 2				

COTTON EYE JOE

Traditional

Arranged by Jan Ericsson, Oban & Pat Reiniz

© Copyright 1994 Zomba Music Publishers Limited, 165-167 High Road, London NW10 2SG. All Rights Reserved. International Copyright Secured.

C#2 16	E2 8	C#2 16	E2 8	C#2 16			TEMPO 125
E2 8	C#2 16	C#2 8	B1 16	C#2 8	- 16	E2 16	C#2 16	C#2 8
B1 16	A1 16	A1 16	F#1 16	A1 8	A1 16	A1 16	F#1 16	E1 8
- 16	D1 16	D1 8	F#1 16	A1 8	F#1 8	A1 16	A1 8	A1 16
D2 8.	- 16	E2 16	C#2 8	C#2 16	B1 8	A1 8	C#2 16	A1 16
A1 8	F#1 16	E1 8					

DRIFTING AWAY

Words & Music by Maxi Jazz & Rollo Armstrong

© Copyright 1996 Warner/Chappell Music Limited, Griffin House, 161 Hammersmith Road, London W6 8BS (50%)/BMG Music Publishing Limited, Bedford House, 69-79 Fulham High Street, London SW6 3JW (50%). All Rights Reserved. International Copyright Secured.

D1 8	A1 8	G1 8	A1 8	F1 8			TEMPO 125
A1 8	E1 8	A1 8	D1 8	A1 8	G1 8	A1 8	A#1 8	G1 8
F1 8	E1 8	D1 8	A1 8	G1 8	A1 8	F1 8	A1 8	E1 8
A1 8	D1 8	A1 8	G1 8	A1 8	A#1 8	G1 8	F1 8	E1 8
D1 8	D2 8	C2 8	D2 8	A#1 8	D2 8	A1 8	D2 8	G1 8
D2 8	F1 8	D2 8	G1 8	D2 8	A1 8	D2 8	D1 8

I BELIEVE

Words & Music by Jeffrey Pence, Eliot Sloan & Matthew Senatore

© Copyright 1994 Tosha Music/EMI April Music Incorporated/Shapiro Bernstein & Company Incorporated, USA. EMI Music Publishing Limited, 127 Charing Cross Road, London WC2H 0QY (66.66%)/Shapiro Bernstein & Company Limited, 8/9 Frith Street, London W1D 3JB (33.34%). All Rights Reserved. International Copyright Secured.

B1	A#1	G#1	A#1	B1			TEMPO
8	8	8	8	8			140

F#2	G#1	B1	F#2	C#2	A#1	F#1	F#2	F#1
4	8	4	4	4	4	8	8	8

B1	E1	B1	F#2	-	F#1	B1	-	D#2
8	8	8	8		8	4.		8

E2	D#2	D#C2	B1	A#1	G#1	A#1	B1	F#2
8	8	8	8	8	8	8	8	4

G#1	B1	F#2	C#2	A#1	F#1	A#1	B1	G#1
8	8	4	4	4	8	8	8	8

E1	G#1	D#2	-	B1
8	8	4	8	2.

I LOVE YOUR SMILE

Words & Music by Narada Michael Walden, Shanice Wilson, Jarvis Baker & Sylvester Jackson Jr.

© Copyright 1991 Gratitude Sky Music Incorporated/Shanice 4 U Music, USA. Carlin Music Corporation, Iron Bridge House, 3 Bridge Approach, London NW1 8BD (90%)/EMI Music Publishing Limited, 127 Charing Cross Road, London WC2H 0QY (10%). All Rights Reserved. International Copyright Secured.

F2	F2	F2	F2	F2			TEMPO
16	8	8	8	8.			90

G2	D#2	F2	-	A#2	A#2	A#2	C3	A2
16	16	8	8	16	8	8	8	8.

G2	F2	F2	-	G#2	G#2	G#2	G2	F2
16	16	8	8	16	8	8	8	8.

D#2	C2	D#2	C2	A#1	-	A#1	D#2	A#2
16	16	8	16	16	2	8	8	8

F2
8

IT'S ALRIGHT

Words & Music by Anthony Mortimer

© Copyright 1993 Bandmodel Limited/Universal Music Publishing Limited,
Elsinore House, 77 Fulham Palace Road, London W6 8JA.
All Rights Reserved. International Copyright Secured.

F1 4	G#1 8	G1 4	F1 4	A#1 4.			TEMPO 125	
G#1 8	G1 4	F1 4.	C#1 4	G#1 8	G1 4	F1 4.	E1 8.	F1 8.
G1 8	F1 2	- 8	D#2 8	D#2 8	F2 8	- 8	D#2 8	D#2 8
F2 8	D#2 8	C2 16	D#2 8	C2 16	D#2 16	C2 16	D#2 8	D#2 8
D#2 8	F2 8	- 8	D#2 8	D#2 8	F2 8	- 8	D#2 8	D#2 8
F2 8	- 8	C2 8	D#2 8	F2 8	G#2 4	F2 4		

LIFE IS A FLOWER

Words & Music by Jonas Berggren

© Copyright 1998 Megasong Publishing Limited/Universal Music Publishing Limited,
Elsinore House, 77 Fulham Palace Road, London W6 8JA.
All Rights Reserved. International Copyright Secured.

A1 8	A1 16	B1 8	D2 8	E2 4.			TEMPO 112	
D2 4	B1 8	B1 8	D2 16	B1 8.	D2 8	E2 16	F#2 8.	F#2 16
E2 8	E2 8.	E2 2	D2 4	- 16	B1 16	B1 8	D2 8	B1 8
D2 8	D2 16	D2 8.	- 8	A1 8	B1 16	D2 8	E2 4.	D2 4
B1 8	B1 8	D2 16	B1 8.	D2 8	E2 16	F#2 8.	F#2 16	E2 8
E2 8.	E2 2	D2 4.	B1 8	D2 8	B1 8	D2 8	D2 16	D2 8.

OUT OF SPACE

Words & Music by Max Romeo, Lee 'Scratch' Perry, Cedric Miller,
Trevor Randolph, Maurice Smith & Keith Thornton

© Copyright 1992 Next Plateau Music Limited/London Music, Griffin House, 161 Hammersmith Road, London W6 8BS (50%)/Charmax Music, Suite B, 2 Tunstall Road, London SW9 8DA (25%)/Universal/Island Music Limited, Elsinore House, 77 Fulham Palace Road, London W6 8JA (25%). All Rights Reserved. International Copyright Secured.

E1 8	F1 8	E1 8	F1 8	E1 8				TEMPO 140
F1 8	G#1 8	A1 8	G#1 8	A1 8	G#1 8	A1 8	G#1 8	F1 8
F1 4	E1 8	F1 8	E1 8	F1 8	E1 8	F1 8	G#1 8	A1 8
G#1 8	A1 8	G#1 8	A1 8	G#1 8	F1 8	F1 4	E1 8	F1 8
E1 8	F1 8	E1 8	F1 8	G#1 8	A1 8	G#1 8	A1 8	G#1 8
A1 8	G#1 8	F1 8						

THE REAL THING

Words & Music by Phil Wilde, Peter Bauwens, Ray Slijngaard & Anita Dels

© Copyright 1994 Decos Publishing, Holland. Universal/MCA Music Limited, Elsinore House, 77 Fulham Palace Road, London W6 8JA. All Rights Reserved. International Copyright Secured.

A1 16	A1 16	E2 16	A1 16	F2 16				TEMPO 125
A1 16	G2 16	A1 16	E2 16	A1 16	E2 16	A1 16	F2 16	A1 16
D2 16	A1 16	E2 16	A1 16	E2 16	A1 16	F2 16	A1 16	G2 16
A1 16	E2 16	A1 16	E2 16	A1 16	F2 16	A1 16	D2 16	A1 16
E2 16	A1 16	E2 16	A1 16	F2 16	A1 16	D2 16	A1 16	E2 16
A1 16	C2 16	A1 16	D2 16	A1 16	B1 16	A1 16		

SET YOU FREE

Words & Music by Michael Lewis, Dale Longworth & Kevin O'Toole

© Copyright 1994 All Boys Music Limited, 222-224 Borough High Street, London SE1 1JX.
All Rights Reserved. International Copyright Secured.

G#1 16	F#1 16	G#1 16	F#1 16	G#1 8				TEMPO 125
F#1 16	G#1 8	F#1 16	G#1 8	C#2 8	C#2 8	G#1 16	F#1 16	G#1 16
F#1 16	G#1 8	F#1 16	G#1 8	F#1 16	G#1 8	C2 8	D#2 8	C2 4
C2 4	C#2 16	C2 16	A#1 4	A#1 4	A#1 4.	C2 16	A#1 16	G#1 4.
C2 4	C2 4	C#2 16	C2 16	A#1 4	A#1 4	A#1 4.	C2 16	A#1 16
G#1 8	C2 8	D#2 8	C2 4					

SWAMP THING

Words & Music by Richard Norris & David Ball

© Copyright 1994 Deconstruction Songs Limited/BMG Music Publishing Limited,
Bedford House, 69-79 Fulham High Street, London SW6 3JW.
All Rights Reserved. International Copyright Secured.

C2 16.	C#2 16	A1 16.	A1 16	A1 16.				TEMPO 160
A1 16	G1 16.	A1 16	A1 16.	A1 16	A1 16.	A1 16	C2 16.	D2 16
A1 16	A1 16	C2 16.	C#2 16	A1 16.	A1 16	A1 16	A1 16	G1 16.
A1 16	A1 16.	A1 16	A1 16.	A1 16	C2 16.	D2 16	A1 16.	A1 16

TELL ME MA

Traditional Arranged by John Hamilton & Philip Larsen

© Copyright 1998 Zomba Music Publishers Limited, 165-167 High Road, London NW10 2SG (80%)/Skin-Rome Music/Leosong Copyright Service Limited, 13 Berners Street, London W1T 3LH (20%). All Rights Reserved. International Copyright Secured.

A1	D2	F#2	F#2	G2				TEMPO
8	8	8.	16	8				125
E2	F#2	F#2	F#2	E2	E2	E2	E2	D2
8	8.	16	8	8	8.	16	8	8
D2	A1	D2	F#2	F#2	G2	E2	F#2	F#2
4	8	8	16	8	8	8	8.	16
F#2	E2	E2	E2	E2	D2	D2	A2	A2
8	8	8.	16	8	8	4	8	8
A2	F#2	G2	G2	G2	G2	-	F#2	F#2
8	8	8	8	16	8	16	8	16
F#2	F#2	D2	D2	C#2	B1	A1		
16	8	8	8	16	8	8.		

THERE'S NOTHING I WON'T DO

Words & Music by Jake Williams

© Copyright 1996 Mute Song, Lawford House, 429 Harrow Road, London W10 4RE. All Rights Reserved. International Copyright Secured.

A1	A1	A1	A1	A1				TEMPO
16	16	8	16	16				125
A1	A1	A1	A1	A1	A1	A1	C#2	C#2
8	16	16	8	16	16	8	16	16
C#2	A1	A1	A1	C#2	C#2	A1	C#2	D2
8	16	16	8	16	16	8	8	8
C#2	C#2	C#2	A1	C#2	C#2	C#2	A1	C#2
16	16	16	8	16	16	8	8	16
C2	C2	C2	A1	D2	A1	A1	A1	A1
16i	16i	16i	8	16	16	16	16	16
A1	D2	A1	A1	D2	E2			
8	8	16	16	8	8			

UP AND DOWN

Words & Music by Danski & DJ Delmundo

© Copyright 1998 Deldan Publishing/Universal Music Publishing Limited, Elsinore House, 77 Fulham Palace Road, London W6 8JA. All Rights Reserved. International Copyright Secured.

A#1 8	- 4	A#1 8	D#2 8	- 8			TEMPO 125
D#2 8	- 8	F2 8	- 4	F2 16	F2 16	F2 8	F2 8	D#2 8
D#2 8	A#1 8.	A#1 16	- 8	F2 16	F2 16	F2 16	F2 8	D#2 8
D#2 8	A#1 8.	A#1 16	- 8	F2 8	F2 8	F2 8	D#2 8	D#2 8
A#1 8.	A#1 16	- 8	A#1 8	G#1 8	G#1 8	C#2 8	C#2 8	A#1 8.
A#1 16								

WE GOT A LOVE THANG

Words & Music by Eric Miller, Chantay Savage & Jeremiah McAllister

© Copyright 1991 Last Song Incorporated/Silktone Songs Incorporated, USA. The International Music Network Limited, Independent House, 54 Larkshall Road, London E4 6PD (50%)/Campbell Connelly & Company Limited, 8/9 Frith Street, London W1D 3JB (50%). All Rights Reserved. International Copyright Secured.

C2 4	C2 8.	G1 16	- 16	G1 16			TEMPO 112
- 16	C2 16	D2 16	C2 16	D2 8	C2 4	C2 8.	G1 16	- 16
G1 16	- 16	C2 16	D2 16	C2 16	D2 16	C2 16	- 16	E1 8
F1 8	E1 16	- 16	E1 8	F1 8	E1 8	G1 8.	- 16	E1 8
F1 8	E1 16	- 16	E1 8	F1 8	E1 8	G1 8.		

AVE MARIA

By Charles Gounod

Based on J.S. Bach's Prelude No. 1 in C Major

© Copyright 2002 Dorsey Brothers Music Limited, 8/9 Frith Street, London W1D 3JB.
All Rights Reserved. International Copyright Secured.

F1 8	A1 8	C2 8	F2 8	A2 8				TEMPO 125
C2 8	F2 8	A2 8	F1 8	A1 8	C2 8	F2 8	A2 8	C2 8
F2 8	A2 8	F1 8	G1 8	D2 8	G2 8	A#2 8	D2 8	G2 8
A#2 8	F1 8	G1 8	D2 8	G2 8	A#2 8	D2 8	G2 8	A#2 8
E1 8	G1 8	C2 8	G2 8	A#2 8	C2 8	G2 8	A#2 8	E1 8
G1 8	C2 8	G2 8	A#2 8	C2 8	G2 8	A#2 8		

BRINDISI FROM LA TRAVIATA

By Giuseppe Verdi

© Copyright 2002 Dorsey Brothers Music Limited, 8/9 Frith Street, London W1D 3JB.
All Rights Reserved. International Copyright Secured.

F1 16	D2 8.	- 16	F1 16	D2 16				TEMPO 50
D2 16	F1 16	D2 16	D2 16	C#2 16	D2 16	F2 8.	- 16	D#2 16
D2 16	C2 32	- 32	C2 32	B1 32	C2 32	D2 32	C2 32	- 32
C2 32	B1 32	C2 32	D2 32	C2 8	A#1 16	F1 32	- 32	F1 16
D2 16	D2 8.	- 16	F1 16	D2 16	D2 16	F1 16	D2 16	D2 16
C#2 16	D2 16	G2 8.	- 16	F2 16	D#2 16	D2 8.	C2 8.	A#1 4

CANON IN D

By Johann Pachelbel

© Copyright 2002 Dorsey Brothers Music Limited, 8/9 Frith Street, London W1D 3JB.
All Rights Reserved. International Copyright Secured.

A2 **8**	F#2 **16**	G2 **16**	A2 **8**	F#2 **16**		TEMPO **90**
G2 **16**	A2 **16**	A1 **16**	B1 **16**	C#2 **16**	D2 **16**	E2 **16**	F#2 **16**	G2 **16**
F#2 **8**	D2 **16**	E2 **16**	F#2 **8**	F#1 **16**	G1 **16**	A1 **16**	B1 **16**	A1 **16**
G1 **16**	A1 **16**	F#1 **16**	G1 **16**	A1 **16**	G1 **8**	B1 **16**	A1 **16**	G1 **8**
F#1 **16**	E1 **16**	F#1 **16**	E1 **16**	D1 **16**	E1 **16**	F#1 **16**	G1 **16**	A1 **16**
B1 **16**	G1 **8**	B1 **16**	A1 **16**	B1 **8**	C#2 **16**	D2 **16**	C#2 **4**

'THE CUCKOO & THE NIGHTINGALE' ORGAN CONCERTO (2ND MOVEMENT)

By George Frideric Handel

© Copyright 2002 Dorsey Brothers Music Limited, 8/9 Frith Street, London W1D 3JB.
All Rights Reserved. International Copyright Secured.

C2 **16**	D2 **16**	E2 **16**	F2 **8**	F2 **8**		TEMPO **140**
F2 **8**	F2 **8**	C2 **4**	D2 **4**	C2 **8**	A#1 **16**	A1 **16**	A#1 **8**	G1 **8**
A1 **4**	D2 **4**	C2 **8**	A#1 **16**	A1 **16**	A#1 **8**	G1 **8**	A1 **4**	- **16**
F1 **16**	G1 **16**	G#1 **8**	G#1 **8**	G#1 **8**	G#1 **8**	G#1 **8**	G1 **4**	A#1 **8**
A1 **4**	G1 **32**	A1 **32**	G1 **32**	A1 **32**	G1 **8**	F1 **4**

1812 OVERTURE

By Peter Ilyich Tchaikovsky

© Copyright 2002 Dorsey Brothers Music Limited, 8/9 Frith Street, London W1D 3JB. All Rights Reserved. International Copyright Secured.

C2 8	F2 8	G2 8	A2 8	G2 8			TEMPO 180
F2 8	G2 8	A2 4	F2 4	F2 4.	- 4	- 8	C2 8	F2 8
G2 8	A2 8	G2 8	F2 4	G2 8	A2 4	F2 4	F2 4.	- 4
- 8	D2 8	G2 8	A2 8	G2 8	D2 8	A#1 8	D2 8	G2 8
D2 8	A#1 8	D2 8	G2 4.	- 4	- 8	C2 8	F2 8	G2 8
F2 8	C2 8	A1 8	C2 8	F2 8	C2 8	A1 8	C2 8	F2 4.

IL TROVATORE: SOLDIERS' CHORUS

By Giuseppe Verdi

© Copyright 2002 Dorsey Brothers Music Limited, 8/9 Frith Street, London W1D 3JB. All Rights Reserved. International Copyright Secured.

F1 2.	A1 8	G1 2.	A#1 8	A1 4.			TEMPO 225
C2 8	F2 4.	D2 8	C2 4.	A#1 8	G1 4.	A1 8	F1 4.	A1 8
C2 4.	B1 8	D2 4.	C2 8	A#1 4.	A1 8	G1 4.	F1 8	G1 4.
A1 8	G1 2	C1 2	F1 2.	A1 8	G1 2.	A#1 8	A1 4.	C2 8
F2 4.	D2 8	C2 4.	A#1 8	G1 4.	A1 8	F1 4.	A1 8	C2 4.
D2 8	C2 4.	A#1 8	G1 4.	A1 8	G1 2.	F1 2.

IMPROMPTU NO.4 IN A♭
By Franz Schubert

© Copyright 2002 Dorsey Brothers Music Limited, 8/9 Frith Street, London W1D 3JB. All Rights Reserved. International Copyright Secured.

G#2 16	B2 16	G#2 16	D#2 16	D#2 16	140
G#2 16	D#2 16	B1 16	B1 16	D#2 16	B1 16	G#1 16	G#1 16	B1 16
G#1 16	D#1 16	A#1 2	G#2 16	B2 16	G#2 16	D#2 16	D#2 16	G#2 16
D#2 16	B1 16	B1 16	D#2 16	B1 16	G#1 16	G#1 16	B1 16	G#1 16
D#1 16	A#1 2

MAZURKA NO. 3 IN F# MINOR
By Frederic Chopin

© Copyright 2002 Dorsey Brothers Music Limited, 8/9 Frith Street, London W1D 3JB. All Rights Reserved. International Copyright Secured.

F#1 8.	G#1 8	F#1 8	A1 8	B1 8	TEMPO 125
D2 16	D#2 16	D2 16	C#2 8.	F#2 8	C2 16	C#2 16	C2 16	B1 8.
F#2 8.	B1 16	C#2 16	B1 16	A#1 8.	C#2 8.	F#1 4	- 16	G#1 8
A1 8	B1 8	A1 16	B1 16	A1 16	G#1 8.	C#2 8.	F#1 4	- 16
G#1 8	A1 8	B1 8	A1 16	B1 16	A1 16	G#1 8.	C#2 8.	F#1 2

PIANO CONCERTO IN A MINOR

By Edvard Grieg

© Copyright 2002 Dorsey Brothers Music Limited, 8/9 Frith Street, London W1D 3JB.
All Rights Reserved. International Copyright Secured.

A3	-	A3	G#3	E3			TEMPO
8	8	16	16	8			90

-	E3	C3	A2	A2	G#2	E2	E2	C2
8	16	16	8	16	16	8	16	16

A1	A1	G#1	E1	E1	C1	E1	F1	G1
8	16	16	8	16	16	8	8.	16

F1	E1	-	E1	F1	F1	G1	E1	-
8	8	4	8.	16	8	8	4	4

G1	A1	B1	A1	G1	-	G1	A1	A1
4	8.	16	8	8	4	8.	16	8

B1	G1
8	4

RHAPSODY IN BLUE

By George Gershwin

© Copyright 1924 (renewed) Chappell & Company Incorporated, USA.
This arrangement © Copyright 2002 Chappell & Company Incorporated. Warner/
Chappell Music Limited, Griffin House, 161 Hammersmith Road, London W6 8BS.
All Rights Reserved. International Copyright Secured.

A2	G2	F2	G2	F2			TEMPO
2.	8	8	8	8			160

G2	F2	E2	D2	C#2	C2	D2	D#2	E2
8	8	8.	8.	8.	4.	8.	8.	4.

C#2	A1	G1	F1	E1	E1	A2	A2	A2
8.	8.	4.	8.	8.	4.	8.	8.	8.

A2	G2	G2	G2	G2	A2	A2	A2	A2
8.	8.	8.	8.	8.	8.	8.	8.	8.

C3	C3	C3	C3	C#3	A2	F#2	G2	F#2
8.	8.	8.	8.	8.	8.	8.	8.	8.

E2	C2	C#2	E2	C#2	A1
8.	8.	8.	8.	8.	4.

SAILOR'S CHORUS FROM 'THE FLYING DUTCHMAN'

By Richard Wagner

© Copyright 2002 Dorsey Brothers Music Limited, 8/9 Frith Street, London W1D 3JB.
All Rights Reserved. International Copyright Secured.

E2 8	D2 8	C2 4	E2 2	D2 4			TEMPO 180
C2 4	F2 8	E2 4	D2 2	F2 4	E2 4	D2 8	G2 - 4
- 4	A2 8	G2 8	- 4	- 8	A2 8	G2 8	- 4 - 4
A2 8	G2 4	E2 8	E2 8	F2 8	E2 4	D2 8	E2 8 D2 8
C2 4	D2 8	E2 8	F#2 4	G2 2			

SWAN LAKE: ACT 1 FINALE

By Peter Ilyich Tchaikovsky

© Copyright 2002 Dorsey Brothers Music Limited, 8/9 Frith Street, London W1D 3JB.
All Rights Reserved. International Copyright Secured.

F#2 2	B1 8	C#2 8	D2 8	E2 8			TEMPO 100
F#2 4.	D2 8	F#2 4.	D2 8	F#2 4.	B1 8	D2 8	B1 8 G1 8
D2 8	B1 2	- 4	B1 4	C#2 4	D2 4	E2 8	F#2 8 G2 8
A2 4.	G2 8	F#2 4	G2 8	A2 8	B2 4.	A2 8	G2 4 A2 8
B2 8	C#3 4.	B2 8	F#2 8	D2 8	C#2 8	B1 8	

AMAPOLA
By Joseph M. Lacalle

© Copyright 1924 Joseph M. Lacalle.
© Copyright 1933 Edward B. Marks Music Corporation, USA.
Campbell Connelly & Company Limited, 8/9 Frith Street, London W1D 3JB.
All Rights Reserved. International Copyright Secured.

A#2 8.	C3 16	A#2 8	G#2 8.	A#2 16		TEMPO 100
G#2 8	G2 4	- 8	C#2 16	D2 8	F2 16	G2 8	A#2 8.	C3 16
A#2 8	G#2 8.	A#2 16	G#2 4	G2 8	- 16	C#2 8	D2 8	F2 16
G2 8	A#2 16	- 8	C#3 16	D3 8	A2 16	A#2 8	E2 16	G2 8
E2 16	F2 8	F1 16	G1 8	F1 16	C#2 8	D2 16	G2 8	F1 16
A#1 8

BOOM BOOM
Words & Music by John Lee Hooker

© Copyright 1961 (renewed) Conrad Music, a division of Arc Music Corporation, USA.
Tristan Music Limited, 22 Denmark Street, London WC2H 8NG.
All Rights Reserved. International Copyright Secured.

A#1 32	B1 32	C2 8.	D#2 16	A#1 8.		TEMPO 140
G#1 16	F1 8.	D#1 16	F1 8	- 8	A#1 4	A#1 4	C2 4	F1 8
- 16	F1 16	G#1 8	A#1 32	C2 32	A#1 8.	G#1 16	F1 8.	D#1 16
F1 8	- 8	A1 4	A#1 4	C2 4	F1 8

FLY ME TO THE MOON (IN OTHER WORDS)

Words & Music by Bart Howard

© Copyright 1954, 1962 & 1973 Almanac Music Incorporated, USA.
TRO Essex Music Limited, Suite 2.07, Plaza 535 King's Road, London SW10 0SZ
for the world (excluding the USA and Canada).
All Rights Reserved. International Copyright Secured.

F2 4	E2 4	D2 8	C2 4	A#1 4			TEMPO 160
C2 4	D2 4	F2 4	E2 4	D2 4	C2 8	A#1 4	A1 2	- 2
- 8	D2 4	C2 4	A#1 4	A1 4	G1 4	A1 4	A#1 4	D2 4
C#2 4	A#1 4	A1 8	G1 4	F1 2	- 4	- 8	F#1 4	G1 8
D2 4	D2 1	- 8	F2 4	E2 4	C2 1	- 4	C#1 4	D1 8
A#1 4	A#1 1	- 8	D2 4	C2 4	A#1 2	A1 2

FRENESI

By Alberto Dominguez

© Copyright 1939 & 1941 Peer International Corporation, USA.
Latin-American Music Publishing Company Limited, 8-14 Verulam Street, London WC1X 8LZ.
All Rights Reserved. International Copyright Secured.

F1 16	G1 8	A#1 16	C2 8	D2 32			TEMPO 100
C2 32	D2 32	C2 16.	A#1 16	C2 8	- 16	C2 8	F2 4	- 4
- 16	D2 16	C2 8	D2 16	C2 8	D2 32	C2 32	D2 32	C2 16.
A#1 16	C2 8	- 16	C2 8	F2 4	- 4	- 16	D2 4	C2 8
A#1 16	A1 8	F1 16	G1 8	- 16	G1 8	D2 4	- 4	- 16
A1 16	A1 8	A1 16	C2 8.	A1 8	G1 2

I'SE A-MUGGIN'

Words & Music by Stuff Smith

© Copyright 1936 Select Music Publications Incorporated, USA.
Campbell Connelly & Company Limited, 8/9 Frith Street, London W1D 3JB.
All Rights Reserved. International Copyright Secured.

C2 4	**-** 16	**D2** 16	**E2** 8	**G2** 8		**TEMPO 140**
- 16	**F2** 8	**-** 2	**-** 8	**C2** 16	**C2** 16	**B1** 16	**A#1** 16	**A1** 8
D#1 16	**E1** 8	**G1** 16	**A1** 8	**C2** 8	**D#2** 8	**C2** 8	**-** 16	**D2** 4
- 8	**-** 16	**C2** 4	**-** 16	**D2** 16	**E2** 8	**G2** 8	**-** 16	**F2** 8
- 2	**-** 4	**-** 8	**C2** 8	**C2** 8	**-** 16	**C2** 16	**C2** 8	**-** 16
C2 8	**C2** 8	**-** 16	**C2** 16	**C2** 4		

MIDNIGHT IN MOSCOW

Based on a song by Vasilij Solovev-Sedoj & Mikhail Matusovskij
New musical arrangement by Kenny Ball

© Copyright 1961 Tyler Music Limited, Suite 2.07, Plaza 535 King's Road,
London SW10 0SZ. All Rights Reserved. International Copyright Secured.

C1 4	**D#1** 4	**G1** 4	**D#1** 4	**F1** 2		**TEMPO 160**
D#1 4	**D1** 4	**G1** 2	**F1** 4.	**C1** 2	**-** 8	**-** 2	**D#1** 4	**G1** 4
A#1 4	**A#1** 4	**C2** 2	**A#1** 4	**G#1** 4	**G1** 2.	**-** 8	**-** 16	**A1** 4
B1 2	**D2** 4	**C2** 8	**G1** 2.	**D#1** 8.	**D1** 16	**D1** 8.	**D1** 16	**C1** 8.
C1 16	**G1** 4	**F1** 8	**G#1** 2.	**-** 4	**A#1** 4	**G#1** 4	**G1** 2	**F1** 4
D#1 4	**G1** 4	**F1** 4	**D#1** 4	**D1** 8	**C1** 2		

PETITE FLEUR

By Sidney Bechet

© Copyright 1952 & 1959 Les Editions Musicales du Carrousel, France.
TRO Essex Music Limited, Suite 2.07, Plaza 535 King's Road, London SW10 0SZ.
All Rights Reserved. International Copyright Secured.

D#1 16	D#1 16	E1 4.	E1 16	E1 16			TEMPO 112
D#1 1	- 8	G1 8.	G#1 8.	A#1 8.	E2 8.	D#2 8.	B1 1	- 8
D#1 4	G#1 8	A#1 8	B1 8	A#1 8	B1 8	A#1 8	G#1 8	A#1 2.
B1 16	C#2 16	D#2 16	C#2 16	B1 2	A#1 2	G#1 1	

TAKE THE 'A' TRAIN

Words & Music by Billy Strayhorn

© Copyright 1941 Tempo Music Incorporated, USA.
Campbell Connelly & Company Limited, 8/9 Frith Street, London W1D 3JB.
All Rights Reserved. International Copyright Secured.

G1 1	- 8	E2 4.	G1 4	C2 4				TEMPO 160
E2 8	G#1 1	- 2	- 4	- 8	A1 1	A1 8	A#1 8	B1 8
E2 8	G1 8	F#1 8	F1 8	D2 8	C2 8	E1 1	- 2	- 4
- 8	G1 1	- 8	E2 4.	G1 4	C2 4	E2 8	G#1 1	- 2
- 4	- 8	A1 1	A1 8	A#1 8	B1 8	E2 8	G1 8	F#1 8
F1 8	D2 8	C2 8	E1 1					

WATERMELON MAN
By Herbie Hancock

© Copyright 1963 Hancock Music Company, USA.
Sony/ATV Music Publishing (UK) Limited, 10 Great Marlborough Street, London W1F 7LP.
All Rights Reserved. International Copyright Secured.

F1 8	C#2 16	- 8	F1 16	C#2 16			TEMPO 70
G1 8.	C#2 16	- 16	G1 8	C#2 16	- 16	F1 8	C#2 16	- 8
F1 16	C#2 8.	G1 16	C#2 16	- 16	G1 8	C#2 16	F2 16	A2 16
A2 16	- 16	F2 16	A2 16	F1 16	C#2 16	G1 8.	C#2 16	- 16
G1 8	C#2 16	F2 16	A2 16	A2 16	- 16	F2 16	A2 16	F1 16
C#2 16	G1 8.	C#2 16	- 16	G1 8	C#2 16

WAVE
Words & Music by Antonio Carlos Jobim

© Copyright 1967 & 1976 Corcovado Music Incorporated, USA.
Westminster Music Limited, Suite 2.07, Plaza 535 King's Road, London SW10 0SZ
for the United Kingdom and the Republic of Ireland.
All Rights Reserved. International Copyright Secured.

E2 8	G2 8	F#2 8	D2 2.	- 8			TEMPO 140
B1 8	C2 8	D#2 8	F#2 8	A2 8	C3 8	B2 4	C3 32	D3 1
- 4	- 8	D3 8	D3 4	E3 8.	D3 8	C3 4	C3 4.	B2 8
C3 4.	B2 8	C3 4	D3 8	B2 1	- 4	B2 8	D3 8	C#3 8
C3 8	B2 4	B2 4	G2 8	G2 8	G2 4	E2 8	G2 8	A2 8
A#2 8	G2 8	F2 8	C#2 8	C2 8	A#1 4	A#1 4	G1 2

ANNA (EL NEGRO ZAMBON)

Music by Roman Vatro Original Words by Francesco Giordano
English Words by William Engvick

© Copyright 1952 Redi Ponti De Lauretiis, Italy. All rights assigned 1952 to Peermusic (UK) Limited for Great Britain, the Republic of Ireland and the British Commonwealth. Latin-American Music Publishing Company Limited, 8-14 Verulam Street, London WC1X 8LZ. All Rights Reserved. International Copyright Secured.

G1 8	G#1 8	A#1 4	C2 8	D2 8		TEMPO 200

D#2 4	F2 8	G2 2	G#2 8	- 4	F1 8	G1 8	G#1 4	A#1 8

| C2 8 | D2 4 | D#2 8 | F2 8 | G2 2 | - 4 | G2 8 | D#2 8 | C2 4 |

| F2 8 | D2 4 | A#1 4 | D#2 8 | C2 8 | G#1 2 | - 4 | F2 8 | D2 8 |

| A#1 4 | D#2 8 | C2 8 | G#1 4 | D2 8 | A#1 8 | G1 2 |

EL WATUSI

Words & Music by Ray Barretto

© Copyright 1963 (renewed 1991) Windswept Pacific Entertainment Company/ Longitude Music Company, USA. Windswept Music (London) Limited, Hope House, 40 St. Peter's Road, London W6 9BD. All Rights Reserved. International Copyright Secured.

A1 4	- 4	D2 4	- 4	E2 4		TEMPO 160

| - 8 | E2 8 | D2 4 | B1 4 | A1 4 | - 4 | D2 4 | - 4 | E2 4 |

| - 8 | E2 8 | D2 4 | B1 4 | E1 8 | E1 8 | F#1 8 | F#1 8 | F#1 8 |

| G#1 4 | G#1 4 | G#1 8 | F#1 4 | F#1 4 | E1 4 | E1 4 | F#1 8 | F#1 8 |

| F#1 8 | G#1 4 | G#1 4 | G#1 8 | G#1 4 | G#1 4 | E1 4 |

GUAGLIONE
By Giovanni Fanciulli

© Copyright 1956 (renewed 1984) Accordo Edizioni Musicali, Italy. Eaton Music Limited, Eaton House, 39 Lower Richmond Road, London SW15 1ET for the United Kingdom, the Republic of Ireland, Australia and New Zealand. All Rights Reserved. International Copyright Secured.

A1 4	G1 8	- 8	- 4	- 16			TEMPO 180
E1 16	A1 4	G1 8	- 16	E1 16	A1 4	G1 8	- 8	A1 4
F1 8	- 8	- 2	F1 8	- 8	F1 8.	F1 16	A#1 4	G1 8
- 8	A1 4	G1 8	- 4	- 8	- 16	E1 16	A1 4	G1 8
- 16	E1 16	A1 4	G1 8	- 8	D1 8			

GUANTANAMERA
Words Adapted by Julian Orbon from a poem by José Marti
Music Adaptation by Pete Seeger & Julian Orbon

© Copyright 1963 & 1965 Fall River Music Incorporated, USA. Harmony Music Limited, Onward House, 11 Uxbridge Street, London W8 7TQ for the British Commonwealth (excluding Canada and Australasia) and the Republic of Ireland. All Rights Reserved. International Copyright Secured.

B2 8	- 8	B2 8	B2 8	B2 8			TEMPO 112
B2 8	- 2	- 4	- 8	G2 8	B2 8	F#2 8	A2 8	- 8
B2 8	F#2 8	A2 8	A2 8	- 1	- 4	F#2 4	G2 8	A2 8
B2 2	A2 2	- 8	B2 8	G2 8	E2 8	D2 8	- 8	D2 8
C#2 8	B1 2	A1 2.						

LA BAMBA

Traditional Adapted & Arranged by Ritchie Valens

© Copyright 1958 Kemo Music Company, USA.
Carlin Music Corporation, Iron Bridge House, 3 Bridge Approach, London NW1 8BD for the British Commonwealth (excluding Canada and Australasia), the Republic of Ireland and Israel.
All Rights Reserved. International Copyright Secured.

G1	A1	B1	C2	-			TEMPO
8	8	8	8	8			140

E2	G2	F2	-	A2	G2	-	G1	B1
8	8	8	8	8	8	8	8	8

D2	F2	F2	E2	D2	C2	-	E2	G2
8	8	8	8	8	8	8	8	8

F2	-	A2	G2	-	F2	F2	F2	F2
8	8	8	8	8	8	8	8	4

F2	E2	-	C2	-	F2	F2	F2	F2
8	8	8	8	1	8	8	8	4

F2	E2	-	C2	-	C2	C2	C2	D2
8	8	8	8	8	8	4	8	8

LA COLEGIALA

Words & Music by Walter Leon

© Copyright 1986 Ollantay Music S.A./Copyright Control.
All Rights Reserved. International Copyright Secured.

D2	D2	D2	A#1	-			TEMPO
8.	16	8	8	16			100

C2	C2	C2	D#2	-	D2	-	D2	-
8	16	8	16	16	16	16	16	16

D2	A#1	-	C2	C2	C2	D#2	-	D2
8	8	16	8	16	8	16	16	16

-	D2	-	D2	-	A#1	-	C2	C2
16	16	16	16	16	8	16	8	16

A1	F1	G1	-	G1	-	G1
8	8	16	16	16	16	2

LAMBADA

Words by Gonzalo Hermosa, Ulises Hermosa, Alberto Maravi, Marcia Ferreira & Jose Ari Music by Gonzalo Hermosa & Ulises Hermosa

© Copyright 1989 & 1991 EMI Songs France SARL/Predisa/BM Productions (45%)/ Adageo, France. EMI Music Publishing Limited, 127 Charing Cross Road, London WC2H OQY (55%). All Rights Reserved. International Copyright Secured.

A1 8.	G2 32	G#2 32	A2 4.	G2 8			TEMPO 125
F2 8	E2 8	D2 8	- 8	D2 8	F2 8	E2 8	D2 8	C2 8
D2 8	A1 8	G1 2.	A1 8	- 16	- 32	- 32	A2 32	G2 4
G2 8	F2 8	A#1 4	A#1 8	D2 4	A2 8	G2 8	F2 8	A#1 4
D2 8	F2 8	E2 8	E2 16	D2 16	C2 8	C2 4	C2 8	D2 8
C2 8	D2 2.

MAS QUE NADA

Words & Music by Jorge Ben

© Copyright 1963 E.M.B.I., S.A., Brazil. © Copyright assigned 1966 to Peer International Corporation, USA. Latin-American Music Publishing Company Limited, 8-14 Verulam Street, London WC1X 8LZ. All Rights Reserved. International Copyright Secured.

D#2 2	C#2 8	C2 4	F2 8	- 4			TEMPO 200
D#2 8	D#2 8	D#2 8	C#2 8	D#2 8	C#2 8	D#2 8	C#2 8	D#2 8
C#2 4	C2 4	F2 8	- 2	D#2 8	C#2 8	D#2 4	D#2 8	C#2 8
D#2 8	C#2 8	D#2 8	C2 2	C2 8	- 8	A#1 8	G#1 8	C2 4
C2 8	E2 4	E2 4	F2 1	- 4	F2 4	G2 4	G#2 4.	F2 4.
A#2 8	G2 4	D#2 8	D#2 8	D#2 8	C2 8	D#2 4	F2 2

OYE COMO VA

Words & Music by Tito Puente

© Copyright 1963 & 1970 Full Keel Music Company, USA.
EMI Music Publishing (WP) Limited, 127 Charing Cross Road, London WC2H 0QY.
All Rights Reserved. International Copyright Secured.

A1 4.	E2 8	G2 8	E2 8	G2 8		TEMPO 125
F#2 4	D2 2	D2 16	C2 16	D2 16	C2 16	A1 16	G1 16	A1 4.
E2 8	G2 8	E2 8	G2 8	F#2 4	A2 2.	- 8	A1 4.	E2 8
G2 8	E2 8	G2 8	F#2 4	D2 2	A1 16	C2 16	D2 16	D2 16
C2 16	A1 16	G1 16	A1 4	C2 8	E2 8	G2 8	E2 8	G2 8
F#2 4	A2 2.							

LA COPA DE LA VIDA

Words & Music by Robi Rosa, Desmond Child & Luis Gomez Escolar

© Copyright 1998 Desmophobia/Universal Music Publishing Limited (41%)/
A Phantom Vox Publishing/Muziekuitgeverij Artemis/Warner/Chappell Music
Limited (41%)/Musica Calaca (18%). All Rights Reserved. International Copyright Secured.

G1 4	G1 4	G1 4.	D#1 8	F1 8		TEMPO 160
F1 8	G#1 8	F1 8	G1 8	- 4	D#1 16	F1 16	G1 8	- 8
G1 8	- 4	G1 8	- 4	D#1 8	F1 16	F1 16	D#1 8	D1 8
D#1 8.	C1 8	- 4	G1 4	G1 4	G1 4	- 8	D#1 8	F1 8
F1 8	G#1 8	F1 8	G1 4	- 8	D#1 16	F1 16	G1 4	G1 4
G1 4	- 8	D#1 8	F1 8	F1 16	D#1 8	D1 8	D#1 8.	C2 8

TEQUILA

Words & Music by Chuck Rio

© Copyright 1958 Jat Music Incorporated, USA.
Universal/MCA Music Limited, Elsinore House, 77 Fulham Palace Road, London W6 8JA.
All Rights Reserved. International Copyright Secured.

B1 8	E2 8	- 8	E2 8	D2 8			TEMPO 180
F#2 8	- 8	D2 8	E2 8	- 2	B1 8	- 2	- 8	B1 8
E2 8	- 8	E2 8	D2 8	F#2 8	D2 8	- 8	E2 8	- 2
- 4	- 8	B1 8	E2 8	- 8	E2 8	D2 8	F#2 8	D2 8
- 8	E2 8	- 8	B1 8	- 2	- 8	B1 8	E2 8	- 8
E2 8	D2 8	F#2 8	D2 8	- 8	E2 8			

TICO TICO

By Zequinha Abreu

© Copyright 1943 Peer International Corporation, USA. Latin-American Music
Publishing Company Limited, 8-14 Verulam Street, London WC1X 8LZ.
All Rights Reserved. International Copyright Secured.

F2 16	E2 16	F2 16	F#2 16	F2 16			TEMPO 140
- 16	A#2 16	- 16	F2 16	E2 16	F2 16	F#2 16	F2 16	- 16
A2 16	- 16	F#2 32	F2 32	E2 16	F2 16	F#2 16	F2 16	D#3 16
C3 16	A2 16	F#2 16	F2 16	D#2 16	C#2 8	- 8	- 16	F#2 16
F2 16	E2 16	D#2 16	- 16	F#2 16	A#2 16	- 16	F#2 16	F2 16
D#2 16	C#2 16	- 16	F2 16	A#2 16	- 4	F2 4	A2 4	A#2 4

TIJUANA TAXI
By Bud Coleman

© Copyright 1965 Irving Music Incorporated, USA.
Rondor Music (London) Limited, 10A Parsons Green, London SW6 4TW.
All Rights Reserved. International Copyright Secured.

A1 16	C2 8	F2 8	E2 8	D2 16				TEMPO 100
C2 8	A#1 4.	G1 16	A#1 8	E2 8	D2 8	C2 16	A#1 8	A1 4.
F1 16	A1 8	D2 8	C2 8	A#1 16	A1 8	G1 4	- 16	G1 16
- 16	A1 16	- 16	C2 16	C2 16	C2 16	- 4	- 8	A#1 8.
A1 8	G1 8	F1 4	C1 4	F1 8				

WHENEVER WHEREVER
Words by Shakira & Gloria Estefan   Music by Shakira & Tim Mitchell

© Copyright 2002 Aniwi Music LLC/Sony/ATV Latin Music Publishing LLC/
F.I.P.P. International, USA. Sony/ATV Music Publishing (UK) Limited, 10 Great
Marlborough Street, London W1F 7LP.
All Rights Reserved. International Copyright Secured.

G#2 16	G#2 8	- 16	G#2 32	- 8				TEMPO 100
- 16	- 32	A2 16	A2 8	- 16	A2 32	- 8	- 16	- 32
G#2 16	G#2 8	- 8	E2 8	F#2 8	G#2 8	F#2 8	E2 8	C#2 8
C#2 16	F#2 32	E2 16.	- 16	E2 8	C#2 8	C#2 8	E2 4	- 8
B1 16	B1 8	- 16	B1 8	D#2 8	B1 8	G#2 4		

ZAMBESI

By Nico Carstens & Anton De Waal

© Copyright 1955 (renewed 1982) Shapiro Bernstein & Company Incorporated, USA.
Shapiro Bernstein & Company Limited, 8/9 Frith Street, London W1D 3JB.
All Rights Reserved. International Copyright Secured.

C1 4.	G1 4.	E1 4	F1 4.	A1 4.			TEMPO 180
F1 4	G1 4.	D2 4.	B1 4	C2 4	- 4	- 8	E2 8	G2 8
C3 8	E3 4	C3 8	D3 4	C3 8	B2 8	A2 8	G2 4	C3 8
E2 4	E2 8	F2 8	F#2 8	G2 8

SAMBA DE JANEIRO

Words & Music by Ramon Zenker, Gottfried Engels & Airto Moreira

© Copyright 1997 Good Morning Music/Bug Music Limited (33.33%)/
Upright Songs Music Publishing/The International Music Network Limited (25%)/
BMG Music Publishing Limited (19.17%)/Copyright Control (22.5%).
All Rights Reserved. International Copyright Secured.

A1 4	C2 4.	A1 8	D2 4	C2 8			TEMPO 160
D2 8	E2 4	C2 8.	A1 16	- 4	A1 4	C2 4	E2 4	A2 4
G2 8	A2 8	B2 4	G2 8.	E2 16	- 4	E2 4	A2 4	E2 4
D2 4	C2 8	D2 8	E2 4	C2 8.	A1 16	- 4	A2 4	C3 4
A2 4	A2 4	G2 8	A2 8	B2 4	G2 8.	A2 1

AULD LANG SYNE

Traditional
Words by Robert Burns

© Copyright 2002 Dorsey Brothers Music Limited, 8/9 Frith Street, London W1D 3JB.
All Rights Reserved. International Copyright Secured.

F1 4	A#1 4.	A#1 8	A#1 4	D2 4			TEMPO 180
C2 4.	A#1 8	C2 4	D2 4	A#1 4.	A#1 8	D2 4	F2 4	G2 2.
G2 4	F2 4.	D2 8	D2 4	A#1 4	C2 4.	A#1 8	C2 4	D2 8
C2 8	A#1 4.	G1 8	G1 4	F1 4	A#1 2

DECK THE HALLS

Traditional

© Copyright 2002 Dorsey Brothers Music Limited, 8/9 Frith Street, London W1D 3JB.
All Rights Reserved. International Copyright Secured.

A1 4.	G1 16	F#1 4	E1 4	D1 4			TEMPO 200
E1 4	F#1 4	D1 4	E1 8	F#1 8	G1 8	E1 8	F#1 4.	E1 8
D1 4	C#1 4	D1 2	E1 4.	F#1 8	G1 4	E1 4	F#1 4.	G1 8
A1 4	E1 4	F#1 8	G1 8	A1 4	B1 8	C#2 8	D2 4	C#2 4
B1 4	A1 2	A1 4.	G1 8	F#1 4	E1 4	D1 4	E1 4	F#1 4
D1 4	B1 4	B1 8	B1 8	A1 4.	G1 8	F#1 4	E1 4	D1 2

DING DONG MERRILY ON HIGH

Words by George Woodward Music: Traditional

© Copyright 2002 Dorsey Brothers Music Limited, 8/9 Frith Street, London W1D 3JB.
All Rights Reserved. International Copyright Secured.

G2 4.	F2 8	E2 8	F2 8	G2 8			TEMPO 200
E2 8	F2 4.	E2 8	D2 8	E2 8	F2 8	D2 8	E2 4.	D2 8
C2 8	D2 8	E2 8	C2 8	D2 4.	C2 8	B1 8	C2 8	D2 8
B1 8	C2 4.	B1 8	A1 8	B1 8	C2 8	A1 8	B1 4.	A1 8
G1 4	G1 4	A1 4	C2 4	C2 4	B1 4	C2 2	C2 2

I CAME, I SAW, I CONGA'D

Words & Music by James Cavanaugh, John Redmond & Frank Weldon

© Copyright 1941 (renewed 1969) Santly-Joy-Select Incorporated, USA. Rights assigned to
Joy Music Incorporated, USA. Campbell Connelly & Company Limited (66.67%)/
Redwood Music (33.33%). All Rights Reserved. International Copyright Secured.

D2 8	D#2 8	D2 8	C2 8	A#1 8			TEMPO 112
C2 8	- 16	C2 8	- 16	C2 8	D2 8	C2 8	A#1 8	A1 8
A#1 8	- 16	A#1 8	- 16	F1 8	G1 4	A#1 4	A1 8.	- 8
- 16	F1 8	G1 4	C2 4	A#1 8.

IN DULCI JUBILO

Composed by Johann Sebastian Bach
Arranged by Mike Oldfield

© Copyright 1975 Oldfield Music Limited.
EMI Virgin Music Limited, 127 Charing Cross Road, London WC2H 0QY.
All Rights Reserved. International Copyright Secured.

C2 **8**	C2 **16**	E2 **8**	F2 **16**	G2 **8**			TEMPO **90**
A2 **16**	G2 **8.**	C2 **8**	C2 **16**	E2 **8**	F2 **16**	G2 **8**	A2 **16**	G2 **8.**
G2 **8**	A2 **16**	G2 **8**	F2 **16**	E2 **8.**	C2 **8**	C2 **16**	D2 **8**	D2 **16**
E2 **8**	D2 **16**	C2 **8**	D2 **16**	E2 **16**	D2 **16**	C2 **16**	A1 **8**	A1 **16**
B1 **8**	B1 **16**	C2 **8.**	G2 **8**	F2 **16**	E2 **8**	E2 **16**	D2 **16**	E2 **16**
D2 **16**	C2 **8.**						

WEDDING MARCH

By Felix Mendelssohn

© Copyright 2002 Dorsey Brothers Music Limited, 8/9 Frith Street, London W1D 3JB.
All Rights Reserved. International Copyright Secured.

C1 **8**	C1 **8**	C1 **8**	E1 **4**	E1 **8**			TEMPO **200**
E1 **8**	E1 **8**	E1 **4**	E1 **8**	E1 **8**	E1 **8**	G1 **4**	G1 **8**	G1 **8**
G1 **8**	G1 **4**	G1 **8**	G1 **8**	G1 **8**	C3 **2**	B2 **4.**	F#2 **8**	A2 **4**
G2 **4**	F2 **4**	D2 **4**	C2 **2**	D2 **4**	G1 **8.**	D2 **16**	E2 **4**	C2 **8**
E2 **8**	G2 **8**	C3 **8**	E3 **8**	G3 **8**	C3 **2**	B2 **4.**	F#2 **8**	A2 **4**
G2 **4**	F2 **4**	D2 **4**	C2 **2**	E2 **4**	D2 **8.**	E2 **16**	D2 **2**	C2 **2**

WE WISH YOU A MERRY XMAS

Traditional

© Copyright 2002 Dorsey Brothers Music Limited, 8/9 Frith Street, London W1D 3JB. All Rights Reserved. International Copyright Secured.

D1 4	G1 4	G1 8	A1 8	G1 8		TEMPO 180
F#1 8	E1 4	C1 4	E1 4	A1 4	A1 8	B1 8	A1 8	G1 8
F#1 4	D1 4	D1 4	B1 4	B1 8	C2 8	B1 8	A1 8	G1 4
E1 4	D1 8	D1 8	E1 4	A1 4	F#1 4	G1 2

HAPPY BIRTHDAY TO YOU

Words & Music by Patty S. Hill & Mildred Hill

© Copyright 1935 (renewed 1962) Summy-Birchard Music (a division of Summy-Birchard Incorporated, USA). Reproduced by permission of Keith Prowse Music Publishing Company Limited, 127 Charing Cross Road, London WC2H 0QY. All Rights Reserved. International Copyright Secured.

G1 4	- 16	G1 8	A1 4.	G1 4.		TEMPO 180
C2 4.	B1 2.	G1 4	- 16	G1 8	A1 4.	G1 4.	D2 4.	C2 2.
G1 4	- 16	G1 8	G2 4.	E2 4.	C2 4.	B1 2	A1 2.	F2 4
- 16	F2 8	E2 4.	C2 4.	D2 4.	C2 2	D2 16	E2 16	F2 16
G2 16	A2 16	B2 16	C3 8

ERICSSON 2618, A1018, A2628, GF768, GF788e, GH688, I888, R250, R310, R320, R380, R380s, R520, S868, SH888

There are four pieces of information for every note in every tune in this book. See your phone's manual for more information on how to access and use the composer mode.

1. Note

2. Sharp

4. Duration

3. Octave

A#2
16

1. Each **NOTE** name corresponds to one of the number keys on your phone (– indicates a **REST**):

1	2	3	4	5	6	7	8	9
C	D	E	F	G	A	B	C+	D+

Key pad equivalent:

Change Octave

Rest   Sharp

2. If the note has a **SHARP** (#) sign after it then press **#**.

3. OCTAVE: Use the **0** key to change the octave of the note. This phone has a range of two octaves – notes in the higher octave are indicated by the + sign.

4. DURATION: Hold down the pitch keys and the length of the note will change. Only two durations are possible: short (indicated by a lower case letter) and long (indicated by an upper case letter). Dotted notes and rests of different durations are not possible.

TIP: Choose tunes with only one or two durations. For example in a tune with durations of 8 and 4, 8 would be entered as a **short** note, and 4 as a **long** one.

ERICSSON

T39M, T66, T68I,
T10, T18, T20e, T20s, T28, T28 world, T29

There are four pieces of information for every note in every tune in this book. See your phone's manual for more information on how to access and use the composer mode.

1. Note — **2.** Sharp

A#2
16

4. Duration — **3.** Octave

1. Each **NOTE** name corresponds to one of the number keys on your phone (– indicates a **REST**):

1	2	3	4	5	6	7	8	9
C	D	E	F	G	A	B	C+	D+

Key pad equivalent:

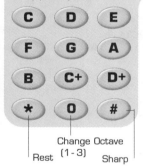

Rest Change Octave (1 - 3) Sharp

2. If the note has a **SHARP** (#) sign after it then press **#**.

3. OCTAVE: Use the **0** key to change the octave of the note. These phones have a range of three octaves.

4. DURATION: Hold down the pitch keys and the length of the note will change. There are four different note lengths except for the **T68i** which supports all six note lengths. Dotted notes and rests of different durations are not possible.

TIP: Choose tunes with up to four different durations, so if the tune has **32** length notes, you can use 4, 8, 16 and 32 length notes. Or if the tune has a **1** length note, you can use 1, 2, 4 and 8 length notes.

SONY CMD-Z5

There are three pieces of information for every note in every tune in this book. See your phone's manual for more information on how to access and use the composer mode.

1. Note — A#2

3. Duration — **16**

2. Octave

1. Each **NOTE** name corresponds to one of the keyboard keys on your phone's screen (– indicates a **REST**):

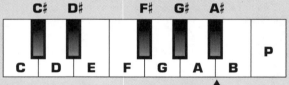

C# D# F# G# A#

C D E F G A B P

▲

Press the jog dial to select a note or press **P** to select a rest (in the diagram above, **A#** is selected). A **SHARP** note will appear lighter than a normal note even though a **SHARP** symbol does not appear.

2. OCTAVE: The default octave is **2**. To change to the lower or higher octaves (**1** or **3**), move the selector arrow below the lowest or highest note on the keyboard – it will then jump to the next octave and will be denoted by an **L** or **H** on the right hand side of the keyboard. If you select a note in a different octave a line will appear below or above the note, e.g: **C1** = <u>C</u>, **C3** = C̄.

3. DURATION: Once you have selected your note pitch and octave (or rest), select the duration and press the jog dial. See the diagram for available note lengths.

1	2	4	8	16
o	♩	♩	♪	♪
▬	▬	♪	♪	♪

NOTE: this phone does not support dotted notes or 32 length notes.

There are four pieces of information for every note in every tune in this book. See your phone's manual for more information on how to access and use the composer mode.

1. Note   **2.** Sharp

4. Duration   **3.** Octave

A#2
16

1. Each **NOTE** name corresponds to one of the number keys on your phone (– indicates a **REST**):

1	2	3	4	5	6	7	-
C	D	E	F	G	A	B	REST

Key pad equivalent:

C   **D**   **E**

F   **G**   **A**

B   **↑**   **↓**

*   **–**   **#**

Change Octave   Shorter Duration   Longer Duration   Sharp

2. If the note has a **SHARP** (#) sign after it then press #. Press # again to cancel.

3. OCTAVE: Use the ⋆ key to change the octave of the note (from 1-3).

4. DURATION: Your phone will stay on the last duration you entered. **Use the 9 key to make the note longer** (e.g. to move from 4 to 2 and then on to 1).
Use the 8 key to make the note shorter (e.g. to move from 4 to 8 and then on to 16 and 32).

If the duration has a dot (•) after it, then hold the original **NOTE** key down for longer, until the note sounds again and • appears on your display.

TEMPO: Go to the options menu and choose tempo from the list.

PRESS 8 ↓   1   2   4   8   16   32   ↑ PRESS 9

123

SAMSUNG A110

There are four pieces of information for every note in every tune in this book. See your phone's manual for more information on how to access and use the composer mode.

1. Note **2.** Sharp

4. Duration **3.** Octave

All information is entered via the **NAVIGATOR** button. To start composing a melody press the **Edit** soft key. Press the **Next** soft key to add a note.

Use the up and down arrows to make the note higher or lower.

Make note **HIGHER (SHARPEN)**

DURATION OF NOTE: hold to alter note lengths.

Enter **REST**: hold for various rest lengths.

Make note **LOWER (FLATTEN)**

TEMPO: this option is not available on this phone.

TIP: this phone can hold up to 100 notes.

DURATION: Refer to the opposite page for a list of available note and rest durations.

OCTAVES : keep pressing the up or down keys until you reach the required octave.

There are four pieces of information for every note in every tune in this book. See your phone's manual for more information on how to access and use the composer mode.

1. Note ——— A#2

2. Sharp

16

4. Duration ———

3. Octave

---

1. Each **NOTE** name corresponds to one of the number keys on your phone (– indicates a **REST**):

1	2	3	4	5	6	7
C	**D**	**E**	**F**	**G**	**A**	**B**

Key pad equivalent:

C **D** **E**

F **G** **A**

B **⇅**

2. If the note has a **SHARP** (#) sign after it then press ⌒ .

3. OCTAVE: Use the **8** key to move up or down one octave.

---

4. DURATION: Press the (key to change the duration.

Available note and rest values:

16	♪	𝄾
8	♪	𝄾
8.	use ♪ + ♪	𝄾 + 𝄾
4	♩	𝄽
4.	♩.	𝄽.
2	use ♩ + ♩	𝄽 + 𝄽
2.	use ♩ + ♩ + ♩	𝄽 + 𝄽 + 𝄽
1	o	–

Change Length Of Note

Up Semitone

( )

Down Semitone

ENTER REST
(press key until the rest is of the required length)

There is no change **TEMPO** option.

125

SAMSUNG N400

There are four pieces of information for every note in every tune in this book. See your phone's manual for more information on how to access and use the composer mode.

1. Note  **2.** Sharp

4. Duration **3.** Octave

A#2
16

1. Each **NOTE** name corresponds to one of the number keys on your phone (– indicates a **REST**):

1	2	3	4	5	6	7
C	**D**	**E**	**F**	**G**	**A**	**B**

Key pad equivalent:

C   D   E

F   G   A

B

↑   –   ↓

2. If the note has a **SHARP** (#) sign after it then press ⌢ .

3. OCTAVE: Use the **8** key to move between three octaves.

Rest

Hold to make note length shorter

Hold to make note length longer

REST: Press and hold key until the rest is of the required length.

4. DURATION:
Press the **(** key to change the duration.

TEMPO: This phone does not support tempo changes or dotted notes.

Up Semitone

Down Semitone

There are four pieces of information for every note in every tune in this book. See your phone's manual for more information on how to access and use the composer mode.

1. Note — **2.** Sharp

A#2
16

4. Duration — **3.** Octave

1. Each **NOTE** name corresponds to one of the number keys on your phone (– indicates a **REST**):

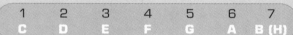

1	2	3	4	5	6	7
C	D	E	F	G	A	B (H)

Key pad equivalent:

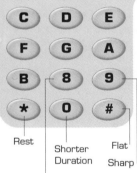

C D E
F G A
B 8 9
* 0 #

Rest — Shorter Duration — Flat / Sharp — Longer Duration

2. If the note has a **SHARP** (#) sign after it then press **9** before you press the note key. Press # again before any subsequent notes to cancel the sharp.

3. OCTAVE: Use the keys to change the octave of the note.

4. DURATION: Use the 8 key to make the note longer. Use the 0 key to make the note shorter. This phone does not support 32 notes, dotted notes or different durations for rests.

TEMPO: This phone does not support tempo changes

SIEMENS c35

There are four pieces of information for every note in every tune in this book. See your phone's manual for more information on how to access and use the composer mode.

1. Note — **2.** Sharp

A#2
16

4. Duration — **3.** Octave

1. Each **NOTE** name corresponds to one of the number keys on your phone (– indicates a **REST**):

1	2	3	4	5	6	7	0
C	**D**	**E**	**F**	**G**	**A**	**B (H)**	**REST**

Key pad equivalent:

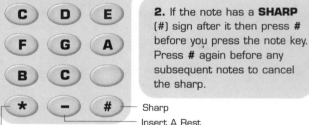

C D E

F G A

B C

* – #

* ——— Sharp
– ——— Insert A Rest

Change Octave

2. If the note has a **SHARP** (#) sign after it then press # before you press the note key. Press # again before any subsequent notes to cancel the sharp.

3. OCTAVE: Use the ✱ key to change the octave of the note. Choose the octave before you press the note key.

4. DURATION: Hold down the note key to cycle through the available tone lengths. This phone does not support 32 notes, dotted notes or different durations for rests.

TEMPO: This phone does not support tempo changes.

TIP: This phone holds a maximum of 49 notes.